Tribulations of My Life

Howard Wallace

Prime Seven Media
518 Landmann St.
Tomah City, WI 54660

Printed in the United States of America

This a breath taking emotional real life story of a young poor African American child with native American genes, growing up in Virginia during the late 50's,which was not an easy time for African American. His mother passed away when he was 5 years old. The story elaborates on the trials and tribulation he went through, trying to survive, on his own, after being separate from his family, ending up living with his ill grandmother. Trying to make his way in the world in a wheelchair the best as he can. You know in the trials and tribulations that life brings. How can I tell what was going through my mind as a child. The biggest tragedy happen in 1999,when he was involved in an traffic accident that left him paralyze from the chest down, with no movements in the upper and lower exstremist. Trying to survive with his disability in a foreign county.

Trials and Tribulations, imperfections in life have molded me for who I am. I came from a broken family but it has somehow molded me to become who I am today. It's a fact I did not have a "perfect" family & I have learnt to accept it after I was adopted by a preacher and his family.

"A journey you want to accomplish begins with one step which is one step forward. Then you keep repeating that step. If you come to an obstacle roll over it and continue on. It won't be easy but later the journey will end and you'll be where you want to be.

(Author: Jill Robinson)

Retrieved 11/5/2013 from-http://www.scrapbook.com/quotes/doc/40237/367.html

TABLE OF CONTENTS

Acknowledgments and Dedication vii

Introduction ix

About Me..1

Who I Am..5

The Beginning 8

It All Begun... 10

Grandma... 16

Uncle Herman.. 19

The Growing Years 23

My Relationships..29

An Ordeal...35

My stay in Germany...38

The Marriage...48

The Accident 58

The Disability...64

How Must I Live? 67

My Boys 69

My Soul was restored...71

The World Today..73

Oh, My God!..88

My Seal..89

My closing remarks 93

ACKNOWLEDGMENTS AND DEDICATION

First, I want to thank you, the reader, for purchasing my very first book. Also, my family and friends, i.e. those that have had a great impact on my life. I would like to thank a number of people and some institutions for making this book possible, particularly my Fellowship supporters. I am forever obliged to God; he encouraged me when my spirit flagged, and never allowed me to doubt my own ability. I also benefited from comments and suggestions from friends and family members. I also want to thank certain individuals who cared and gave me the boost I needed. They asked me to include the fact that the Lord is healing you through our prayers. I must personally thank, Rev. Dan Alewine and his lovely wife, Colette. Who returned to the United States back in 2002. I miss their spiritual advice and teaching because, I know God sent them into my life when I had just about given up.

I also dedicate this book especially to my children, Howard Wallace Jr., Marcel Wallace, Jamie Markowitz, and my grandson "Mike". In the hope that one day they will never undergo the things that I did and that they will realise, the things about life that I always was preaching to them over and over again. I hope that all my real and trusted friends and all the people that know me and the way I am. For everyone who reads this book will see, that nothing in life is free, if you do not have faith in God. Remember, there is nothing more you can do to turn your children's hearts closer to yours than by keeping a journal of your personal history. Ultimately, your children will know about your successes and failures.

It took me this long to see that the Lord had a mission for me. You have to give something in order to receive. He restored my soul and gave me a second chance. And I am taking advantage of that chance and doing his will.

I would also like to dedicate this book to my biological sister and brother wherever they may be today, Mary Little, Jane, Pricilla, Gary, and Edward Robert Walker Jr. (decease) Also to my adopted family, who rescued me: Mary Wallace, Joann Wallace, Willie Wallace and the Rev. Summerfield Wallace Jr.(Decease 2012) and, finally, to the most important person of all: she is now deceased but in my heart she is still alive; Mrs Wilhelmina Turpin Wallace,(was a real mother to me). Passed away July 2, 1996.

INTRODUCTION

*W*henever I saw an old green pick-up truck pulling into grandma's driveway, grand ma would send me out to play with my tricycle. This was a Christmas present given to me by a white man named "Jake "I had to call him ,Mr. Jake, who, I found out later he was dating my grandmother "Sarah". He would show up once or twice a week. I use to see him, secretly passing her money, before he left. My grand ma, used to make me sit on his lap in which I hated, because he always wanted me to play with his testicle. He always wanted me to kiss him, and play with his tonque. What should I do? I guess I was around four or five years old back then. Today, I am a filthy-three-year old African -American, whose life story, I believe, is worth telling. How did I get to live with my grandmother? Well first let me give you the definition of a parent: a father or mother; one who brings forth or one who gives birth to or nurtures and raises a child; a relative who plays the role of guardian.

My so-called parents could not bear living together anymore and inevitably we the innocent children became the victims of the situation. We lived in a small area back in the woods called *"Over the Hill."* Now, let me tell you a little about Over the Hill. Well, as far as I can recollect, it was a great distance back in the woods in a small county called Chester County, Virginia, USA. We lived close to the railroad tracks, where trains were constantly coming and going.

There were around twelve houses, better known as 'shacks'. The population was around 50, predominant poor black people, mostly relatives. The main highway was made of red clay and when it rained it would be very muddy and slippery, and when it was dry, it was very dusty. However, we use to like to eat clay occasionally because it had a sweet and sour taste, and the older people said it is healthy and protects you from bacteria. Sometimes when it rained we would go out and make mud houses because it was very slippery. The only white people that would drive through were either the Sheriff, looking for some black person that has broken the law. During hunting season, the game warden that would come and check whether or not you had hunting or fishing permit.

The ambulance or Rescue Squad would occasionally come through to pick up someone who was very ill or who had just been shot or died. Red Cross would come once a year to vaccinate all of the children and old folks. To go to school we had to pass through the predominately white neighborhood because, the bus would not pick us up in the area where we live. We were not allowed to walk on the main road; we had to take the path through the woods so that we would not be seen by anyone. The white people were sometimes nice to us, only if we did not step over their boundary. After Thanksgiving, or Christmas our parents who was working for them, would pick up the leftovers from the turkey or ham, and bring it home to us. Once in a while we received old clothing from their children, which they would otherwise have been thrown away. We were also not allowed to play with white children, and white kids were not allowed to go past our vicinity alone. I remember one time in the summer, a white boy rode pass on his bike and we all ran out of our shacks to see him. Back then, I did not know the meaning of prejudice but I remember that when we were sick, the white doctor would come to us only when he had time, or later in the evening after closing hours. This was because it was not considered appropriate for us to go to his office. Once, I had to be rush to the hospital, because of bleach poising. My cousin played a trick on me, my cousin Charles, gave me a glass of bleach with ice cubes, and told me that it was only lemonade. In the hospital there, they had to pump the bleach out of my stomach, and after two hours, they sent me home, because I was not allow to stay overnight. Regardless of the crazy and dangerous things we did, we were never bored. There was always something to do. Either we would build a tree house, or a go-cart, or just tease the cats and dogs by setting fire to their tails. But my hobby was climbing trees. Yes, I loved to climb to the top of the trees and jump into the next like a daredevil. I was very active and played on my own most of the time. My real name is Howard Walker but that changed after I had been adopted .I was the smallest child in the family, my father gave me the name 'romp'. Romp is someone or something that runs easily and fairly fast. However, my father's definition was different. He compared me with a baby pig. In other words I was the black sheep of the family. Furthermore, believe me he used to make me feel as though I was. When I misbehaved he would make me go into the woods and get my own strap (switch). As you continue to read you will see that this is a breathtaking, bitter-sweet story about me.

ABOUT ME

Sometimes when I'm alone I cry, because I am on my own. The tears are warm but bitter. They flow with life but take no form. I cry because my heart is torn. I find it difficult to carry on. If I had someone to confide in and share my misery, I would cry among my treasured friends, but who do you know that stays that long in order to help another person carry on? The world moves fast and it would rather pass by. To stop and see what makes one cry is so painful and sad. And sometimes... I cry and no one cares.

Life is like a school. We move through it and learn many things. Losing ourselves in knowledge of our environment we enter this earth like a giant piece of smashed mirror, every one of us reflecting the light of our god.

I am an Afro-American, with native Indian roots. My complexion is coffee-brown; I 'am 5 feet 7 inches tall, very sporty built. I graduated from high school in 1976. I was not one of the smartest of all, but my grades were good enough to ensure I graduated. When I graduated I received the Citizenship of the Year award. The Citizenship of years was awarded only to indivuals who committed their free time by doing community services. In high school I was a member of different organizations such as the Alpha Beta Delta club, the 4-H Club, theatre, and the School Marching Band. In sports I was twice district champion, three times regional champion and came in third place in the State Wrestling Championship. In1982 I was initiated into the Masonry Lodge. In the 10th grade I earned a scholarship for the Blacksmith Institute for Agriculture, but I didn't go. Instead, I joined the Arm forces.

In social affairs I tend to wait for others to introduce themselves; when I am attracted to someone I prefer to be the one pursued. I am most comfortable by myself. In my relationships, I do not make most of the decisions, I believe in a 50/50 relationship. I love it when people speak to me and hate it when people talk badly about others behind their back.

Before I reveal more about myself I would just mention, for any of my readers who are interested in astrology, that I am an Aries. I am not too deep in astrology but just for the record I suppose to have an Aries type of personality. That's why I want to share with you what I research on the Internet. According to an article I found: 'The Aries is guided by flashes of intuition and irresistible impulse. He is a fiery dynamo who is driven by a constant desire to forge ahead into new territories.

When the Aries sets his sights on a goal, it becomes an all-enveloping quest. The Aries native never gives up, but moves ever forward with an obstinate force of will. Like all fire signs, he constantly feels vital energy pushing through him, and he must use that energy or burn up.

'Aries strives for independence, and success is defined by a series of distinctive or high-reaching personal achievements. Coming in first or accomplishing the impossible are the ultimate goals. Athletes, entrepreneurs, soldiers, doctors, religious leaders, race car drivers and explorers are all associated with this sign. Aries does not fear danger, and accidents are all too common with this sign, particularly head injuries.

'If the Aries seems brusque or disinterested it is because his mind is set on a goal that entirely absorbs his energy. Anything that interferes becomes an annoying distraction. Once the Aries sets his sights on someone or something that becomes an urgent and immediate priority. If you are that goal, you can be sure that you will be showered with a love that burns as bright as the sun, and you can expect to be blessed with the greatest fire of devotion.'

What more can I say? It's an exact description of me. Do you want to know how to treat me? Well, Aries is a highly intuitive, fiery, fast-acting, independent person who above all needs his freedom. Aries people can stand alone in the world, and take pride in their ability to go through life without depending on others. They always have a plan of action. If the Aries person is not moving fast physically, you can safely assume that his mind is swimming with ideas. For Aries, the head is what it's all about, and Aries wants to put every idea into practice.

So how do you treat someone who doesn't appear to need anyone? First of all, let your Aries person know how wonderful and special she/he is. In spite of the bold, confident appearance, that person is probably a loner. Also, they may never really feel complete or accomplished at anything because of the high standards they set for themselves. So praise them in order to boost their ego. And offer your loving support and encouragement to fan their passionate fire.

Second, allow them to follow their dreams, and offer helpful pointers and solutions wherever needed. You might feel invisible and unappreciated, but don't despair. They feel as if you are a part of them, and therefore may not understand the need to show gratitude. Just notice the way they glow when you give your advice, or the loving looks you receive. They will have been inspired to do even more. To an Aries, that is the biggest thank you of all.

Most importantly, do everything possible to make him or she feels unfettered. Like all fire signs, they can't stand to be bossed around or confined – unless it is a means to an end. Let them come up with the idea first, if possible. Otherwise, if you want them to do something, ask gently!

The Aries person has a passionate heart and the best of intentions, yet is a very sensitive individual. Your thoughtful love will be rewarded with heroic effort on their part. As Paul Harvey used to say: "Now, you know the rest of the story. "

WHO I AM

*E*very one of us has a story to tell as well as a sacred duty to preserve and pass it on. This is in addition to keeping alive the stories and memories of those who have gone before us. The following indicates who I am:

This is what I've done with my life so far.
This is what I'm doing now.
This is what I believe and think about things in life.
These are world events that shaped my life and generation.
This is what I plan and hope to do in the future.
These are the people (family and friends) who have
had and still have an impact in my life.
And so on!

Who am I? Have you ever asked yourself these questions? If so, you should know:

You are a child of God – a daughter or son of your
Heavenly Father, who knows you and loves you.
You lived with your Heavenly Father before you were born.
He has known you and loved you from the beginning.

*You are created in the image of God. Your Heavenly Father has
created this world for you to learn, to grow, and to become like
Him. Eventually, you can return to live with Him forever.
For this purpose, He has sent His Son into the world. Through
the Saviour, nothing can separate us from the love of God.
You are a child of God and He loves you. This is your
oldest, deepest, and most basic identity.*

Where did I come from?

*You didn't suddenly spring into this earthly existence. You were happy in
His presence, but He knew that you needed more in order to progress. You
did not have a physical body like you do now, and you needed a chance to
gain experience on your own, away from His presence, but with the ability
to communicate with Him and receive help. So He sent you to Earth, hoping
that you would return to Him and receive everything He has to offer you.
Before you were born, you lived with your Heavenly Father as one of His
beloved spirit children. You knew and loved Him, and He knew and loved you.
Although you have forgotten your life before you were born,
your Heavenly Father has not. He knows you and loves you.
He wants you to come to know and love Him, too.*

Why am I here on this planet?

*You are not here by accident. There is a purpose for your mortal
existence. You are here to receive a physical body, gain experience,
and develop divine attributes such as justice, mercy, and love.
God did not send you here without a plan. His plan is designed
to bring you, and all His children, greater peace in this life
– no matter what its trials – and eternal joy in the life to
come. It is a plan of eternal salvation and happiness.*

What is the purpose of life? Have you ever thought there must be something more to life than just living from day to day?

There is much more. Your life has a divine purpose. God, your heavenly Father, has prepared a marvellous plan for your happiness. When you realise that God has a plan for you, it is easier to understand why you are on this Earth. God wants all of His children to progress and become more like Him. This time on Earth provides opportunities for you to grow and progress. Coming here allows you to receive a physical body, exercise agency and learn to choose between good and evil.
Learn and gain experience that will help you
become more like your Heavenly Father.
By carrying out our Heavenly Father's plan, you, like all of His children, can someday return to live with Him and with your loved ones. You can have greater peace in this life and eternal joy in the life to come. Now that is beautiful. That's what I am: I'm someone waiting for Judgement Day.

The Beginning

*L*et me introduce you to my story by telling you of a family feud we had. I had two brothers and three sisters: Pretoria, Maryann, Susan, Leroy,Robert (my oldest brother Robert recently died recently from cancer, I am told). My father was James and my mother Martha .

My younger brother Leroy was always in and out of boys' homes until he turned 18 then he was finally put in prison. I was told they gave him 75 years for robbery. He allegedly robbed an old man and somehow broke his back in the process. My brother Robert moved to New York and got married to Sheila. My sister Maryann use to 'see' things, she was always scared. For instance, she would tell us she'd seen a man with no head! Maybe it was because my uncle used to tell us a scary story about a man with no head. In the summer nights we would all gather around an old oak tree and he'd tell us stories, sometimes until midnight. Other nights he'd take us through the woods to the railroad tracks and tell us about how the slaves were killed. I used to be so scared that I couldn't get to sleep at night and didn't even dare to go to the toilet. Occasionally, I would wet the bed and this would lead to my mother and father getting angry with me. It got so bad that one day my father threatened to kill our uncle because he was always tell us scary stories.

I loved to be around my granddaddy because he taught me so many things about life and what I would have to expect as a black kid growing up in this prejudiced country. He also taught me many tricks, such as how to catch a catfish and hunt deer and racoons. The only thing he was afraid of was snakes but all blacks are scared of snakes and deep water.

I remember one day he screamed in terror. "HOWARD!" he shouted to me. "A snake is in my bed!" I was so scared because it was a big black snake; it was thick and about six feet long. I didn't know what to do so I screamed for my grandma and she came running with a big stick. She killed the snake and then she fed it to the pigs. I never saw a snake as long as that in my whole life and believe me, since that day I am very scared of all snakes. I remember one day I was playing in the trees when I saw a harmless green snake. That was the last time I climbed that tree!

On Sundays we had to go to church with my grandmother and grandfather. The best thing I liked about going to church was that after the church service there would be a picnic with lots of food. I think just about everyone brought something to eat or drink. There was chicken, potato salad, yams, cornbread, just about everything you can think of. The picnic was followed by a game of softball which would last until around 4 o'clock. At 6 o'clock the evening revival service began which for me was as boring as the service. I spent most of my time alone, although I had one friend we called "Chucky. He had two sisters Wanda and Jill. His father was a baker and his mother used to be a photographer although it was just a hobby of hers.

I cannot mention everyone to start with because this only the Introduction. As you read my story you will get to meet each person who at some time or another has played some kind of role in my life. Welcome to my life story. I hope you will enjoy reading it.

IT ALL BEGUN

A child's penetration is keener, and a child's judgment is fairer, than most parents imagine. It is true that a child's knowledge is limited, and that therefore he can be easily turned aside from inquiry into a realm of facts with which he is quite unacquainted. Now saying that,

It all began on March22, 1958 somewhere in Chesterfield, County Virginia. That's the year I suppose to have come into this world. As of today I cannot verify my exactly date of birth, mainly we was not born in a hospital but by a midwife. I picture myself as a poor little black boy with dirty trousers, and holes in the bottom of my shoes. I later on in my life learn that Black Americans faced many disadvantages during the1950's. In short they were discriminated; from public services, and restaurants. After the American Civil War in 1865, black people in the American south were no longer slaves. But they had never gained equality with whites. Blacks had remained second classed citizens throughout their movement to America, with the worst paid unskilled jobs in farms and factories. But I as an innocent child I grow up with no ideas about life or what to expect. Indeed, I didn't even know my name until I was told later in life. I didn't know the color of my skin, the color of my hair or the color of my eyes. No one informed or told me these things. As a child, things were happening around me without me having any idea of what was going and on. On one occasion I was beaten by my grandmother because I was playing with a little white boy whose family was as poor as ours. Anyway, she ran out of the house and grabbed me as if I had killed somebody. But at that time I did not understand why. I also remember with that same little white boy and I were playing together on a go-cart that we had built together. I was pushing him down the hill and we were having the time of our life. The more he laughed, the faster I would push. Then, something happened to me that I will never, ever forget. His older brother I, suppose back then he was around 12 years old and I was around 6. Anyway, his brother ran out of the house with hate in his eyes and hit me with his fist, in the mouth. He began to shout and call me all kinds of names, and then threatened to shoot me with his father's shotgun. His mother and sister all stood there on the porch and watched. I could not understand what I had done wrong. Later, I realized that as I was pushing the go-cart, there was part of a nail sticking in his back and he was crying. I mistakenly thought he was having fun; my reward was a busted lip. I went home feeling depressed and empty; my lip was swollen for something that had happened by accident. That was the very first bad incident that I experienced as a Negro in my childhood. My parents were separated when I was still very young. My father was always coming home drunk and never had a steady job, the sheriff was always picking him up for this or that. Actually, they were always picking up some black person in the neighborhood. I remember Every Friday night, a tall black man would come through the neighborhood, and he had a walking cane, sometimes he would give us Mary Jane and tootsie rolls (sweets) and always had a brown bag with him. On one occasion my brother had a fight with him and so did my father. I was told that the police were constantly on the lookout for him but, I remember my mother liked him. Most of the time he would come by when my father was not home and we had to go out and play. Although I was just a kid, I had a strange feeling that there was something evil about that man. Everyone called him the Candy man.

When my mother died. It was said she was taking some kind of drugs that he had been giving her, but I don't know what became of him.

Before she died I was with her all the time and accompanied her wherever she went. My sister Maryann and Pretoria and Susan moved to my Aunt Helen's house, she lived on the other side of town. I was taken to my grandma Sarah. My mother's mothers who live on the other side of the county called Columbus Heights. It had a small population, consisting predominated poor blacks. We lived near the main highway that ran through a big industrial area called Mack's Chemical Company. The funny thing about this neighborhood was that the Church for black people was located directly in the white neighborhood and the White Protestant Church was located directly in the poorest black neighborhood! What do you make of that? I mean, back then I didn't understand it either, the only thing that was very important for all of us black children was that we had to respect every white person by saying, "Yes sir, yes, ma'am "and we were not allowed to look them in the eyes. But my grandmother had great deal of respect for them; she was more like an Uncle Tom towards them. However, she was always getting rewards and food. Once, she introduced me to one of her so call house friends, his name was Mr. Jake. He had a green pick-up truck and was aged around 40 years old. Also, he was fat and always had jeans and a blue plaid shirt and cowboy booths, and wore a green John Deere cap most of the time. I always had to sit on his knee and he wanted me to touch him in his groin before he left. He would also ask me to touch his tongue with mine and reward me by giving me a bag of jelly beans. Often when I saw him coming I would go next door to play with my friend pooh pooh Once, I told my friend's father about it and they were very angry. They talked to my grandma but she punished me for telling someone about what was going on. I didn't understand why. My mother also had a big argument with my grandmother after I had told my mother I was scared of the man. Anyway, because of all of these incidents my mother decided that it would be better if I went with her. She used to take me just about everywhere with her. I was living like a gyspy boy, one night here, the next night there. I had to spend many nights with people who did not wanted me in their home. One night, a friend of my mother was trying to comb my nappy hair and I was crying in pain because my hair was nappy and dry. Another time I had ringworm on my head and my mother was not around to take me to the doctor. Her friend, who was watching me, was afraid that her children would also get ringworm so she took me in the middle of the night to a ,"Do drop Inn' bar where my mother was working as a waitress and left me there. The owner of the bar said to my mother, "I'll take him upstairs to my room so that he can sleep. I was so scared and begin to cry but she slapped me and told me to shut up. He took me somewhere in a back alley, it was very dark and cold there, and he left me. I was so afraid and cold that soon or later I fell asleep. I woke up the next day because it was cold and I was very hungry. I heard cars and music and drunken people fighting around me. My body was covered in leaves, that I use to keep me warm. And I realized that I had spent the night in a ditch across the street from the bar. The screaming and fighting was my mother being beaten by the owner of that bar because she was looking for me. Afterwards, she brought me back to my grandma to stay. She promised me that she would never leave me alone again but she did, again and again and again. The last time I saw my mother was at her funeral, she was in a lavendar-coloured coffin. She was wearing a light blue nightgown. It's hard to hold back the tears as I write because although my mother gave me so little I still loved her and that hurts the most. She was not there when I needed her most, and she is not here now as I suffer with my handicap. She was not there when I started school; she was not there when I hurt my knee and cried out for her. Oh, God, where is she? The funeral, well I still can see it as if it were yesterday. It was the worse day of my childhood. I cried, my sisters and brothers cried, my father was there. I think there were many, many people there. I remember how I approached her coffin, and wanted to wake her up because I did not understand why she was sleeping so peacefully. That night when I was alone she came to me in my room, she said, "Howard, I'm sorry that I had to leave you this way but, my son, I will always be with you. Do well to all, and the Lord will always open the door for you. The next day I told my grandmother and the first thing she did was cry. Then she took me in her arms and held me so tightly, I thought that she would never let me go. Then she said, "Praise to the Lord. " Later, as I was adjusting to life and becoming a young boy, I never forgot my mother. My mother's brother, Uncle Nate, was trying to be a father to me but he was not often at home, he was a bus driver, and was always on the road, sometimes week at a time. My grandma was too old to play or to teach me things after my mother passed away. I didn't have much contact with my sister or brothers or with my father. I don't know if my father is dead or alive but I do know that my brother Leroy, was still alive and incarcinated.I had to learn a lot on my own. I had to escort my grandma to church every evening during revival service. Every Sunday at 10 am in the morning we went to Sunday school. From 3 pm until 6 pm, in the afternoon we attended regular service. At first, always being alone was sometimes very boring because during the day I didn't see any children. I think they were in school but I wasn't. Although my mother was dead I felt that she was near me.I would tell her everything I did, I even told her how I was trying to destroy a wasp's nest and how I got stung everywhere, and you know what? She used to answer me by saying, "I know, I saw it too." Also, because of my being alone, I was always talking to God. He was a very good listener. I spent a lot of my time walking and playing in the woods. I even got lost a couple of times but the Lord guided me back to safety. I hated Friday nights because at 7pm, the KKK's always had their revival ceremony and part of the ceremony was to burn the cross. One time I forgot that it was Friday and was outside playing when they marched by. Oh, man, I was so scared that I hid behind a tree until they passed. My grandmother was going crazy because she did not know where I was, because normally you would not see any black kids on the streets at that time. Because they hid in their homes. After the KKK's had passed by, I ran home, and that was the first time that my grandmother whipped my backside. Later she explained why she did it and that made me wiser. And that's how my life all began.

GRANDMA

*L*et me tell you about my grandmother. Other than my mother, she was my favourite girl. My grandma was an expert at cooking soul food. I remember waking up at her house to the comforting smells of breakfast. The best times of my childhood were when I was living with my grandmother who was a native of Virginia. Breakfast at her house included bacon, salt pork, scramble eggs, homemade biscuits, original brown gravy, fried potatoes, grits and many other goodies that were guaranteed to fill the table.

In the spring and, in the summer I recall the sweet smell of flowers and how the birds sang in the trees. I also loved the smell of autumn. Particularly the wonderful smell of floral leaves, and the sun shining through the trees, the farmers gathering their ripened crops as they prepared for winter. Once I went with my neighbour and their children to a Halloween party. It was pretty cool to ring people's doorbells and then say the magic words "Trick or Treat". I didn't know what it meant but it seemed to work.

The people would give us candies, apples, oranges, etc. My bag would was very full. Afterwards we would go home and my grandmother would open and check each piece of candies, to see if anyone had put poison in them. There were many incidents where little children were given poison in their candies, particularly on Halloween night. In the winter it was very cold. Sometimes it would snow for days. On one occasion there was so much snow that the weight of it cause our roof fall in and there were piles of snow in the house. Back then we did not have a telephone or a TV. We only had a radio. My grandmother would send me to the neighbours to ask for help because she was too old and weak to shovel snow, and I was too small. When I opened the door the snow was so high, that I couldn't walk out of the house.

I will never forget that one winter, where it was so cold and we only had an old wooden stove. I had to go out and collect wood which wet and piled up outside in the back yard. Have you ever tried to burn wood that is wet? Believe me, it's a waste of time, it can't be done. I think that I slept under three pounds of blankets that my grandmother made that night. You know, black people always try to keep warm in the winter. We an outhouse which was the toilet in the back of the house. Because grandma was too old and weak to outside, I had to empty her besdpan. For those who do not know what a bedpan is, a bedpans and urinals are devices that allow a person in bed to urinate or have a bowel movement (BM).

Around Christmas time we would enjoy ourselves as best we could. We never had a Christmas tree, but I still believed in Santa Claus. I always believed that he would come down the chimney, with lots of presents. I really cannot say too much about Christmas with my grandmother, because I don't remember all the details. But I do know it was not the typical Christmas where all the family came together and celebrated the birth of Jesus Christ. For me it was just another winter and survial was more important. I also remember that it was only my grandmother and I, and that's why I always loved my grandma, because she was my favourite girl in a manner of speaking. It was also another experience in my life as a child. After my family and I were separated we lost all contact with one another.

I didn't ask my grandma about my sister or brothers, I think they never looked for me. When spring arrived my grandmother was often very sick, but what could I do for her other than hold her hands and pray with her? Somehow I knew that she wanted die, I could feel it in my heart. She would sit there and stare out of the window, sometimes for hours. She was always singing that old black gospel hymn, "Precious Lord, take me home, I am tired and weak." I used to cry to see her in so much distress. Back then I was only a lonely little black boy, with little meaning to my life. But I knew what feeling was. Today I know what suffering and grieving means. Even today dealing with my handicap, sometimes I sit and stare out of the window, and begin to cry to myself and ask the Lord to have mercy on me. I never knew when my grandmother died. Recently, I was browsing through the Internet on a website called "Family Tree". I typed her name in the people search and found she passed away 17 years ago. As I look back now from an adult's perspective, I realize how lonely she must have been without Grandpa.

Sadly, I was unable to make it to her burial because no one informed me that she passed away. But I am content; she is resting in peace in God's paradise. She lived a life of hardship, slavery and depression. She had a warm heart and was very religious and was the one who taught me about our father which are in heaven. Through her teaching, I went to church every Sunday. Through her I now know how to make my own decisions and not to call everyone who smiles at you your friend, because evil has many faces.

UNCLE HERMAN

*B*ecause my grandma was to old and weak to take care of me, I was taken to the next of kin – who happened to be my mother's brother, Uncle Herman – and Aunt "May. They lived in a county called Charles City, which was situated far back in the woods. Indeed, it was so far back that you could not hear the cars passing by on the main road. Let me tell you a little about my Uncle Herman and Aunt May. He was about my current age, around 45-50 years old. He didn't have a job as he was injured during the Vietnam war. He lost two fingers and suffered from shellshock. Every month, he would receive his Disability pension check, from the Army then drive to Richmond ,which was about 30 miles away. where he would do his shopping. Then he would make his daily stop at the ABC store to purchase his bottle of whiskey and a bottle of wine. Sometimes he would treat me well, but on other occasions he would be bad tempered. I never knew why, but I think that it had something to do with the Army. Aunt May, was around 88 years old and half blind; she had cataracts on her eyes and could hardly hear.

She never went outside. Just now and again to the porch. Also, she never called me by my name – maybe she never *knew* my name. She would shout, "Hey, Boy!" whenever she wanted or needed something. "Bring me this!" she would demand, or "bring me that!"

From time to time I would just ignore her. She couldn't hear that well either and you had to shout at her. My uncle used to bring her sweets, although she didn't have any teeth to eat them with. And she was very stingy. She would hide her sweets under the mattress, sometimes under her pillow. Uncle Herman would hide his whiskey and wine under the house, which was a very old two-storage house with three bedrooms. In the back, he built a smoke house and there he would smoke meat and salt herrings. In the springtime, my uncle and I would whitewash the house down with lime. Now don't ask me why, because back then I didn't know, and today I still don't know why. My uncle was very active; he used to cut the grass, fix the roof, plough the garden, wash his car, just about anything you can think of. And do you know what? He taught me everything about planting butter beans, snaps, corn and how to cultivate. Later on in high school I won a scholarship to go to a blacksmith institute for agriculture. I was even on TV with the Four Leaf Club but agriculture wasn't my thing.

Each day was full of adventure. My day would begin around 10am; I'd eat breakfast before feeding the pigs. Then I would go in the woods and play because there were no other children to play with. This meant I would spend my day playing alone. In the late evening I would chase down and catch butterflies or June bugs then I would tie a piece of thread to their legs and let them fly away. Around 8 or 9pm I would catch fireflies, put them in a jar and use them as a flashlight. Sometimes I would catch grasshoppers because my uncle told me they give out honey. We never had too many visitors although every blue moon my Aunt Helen would visit and bring me clothes and check me to see if I was keeping okay. She was the aunt who lived with my two sisters, Maryann and Pretoria.

I remember one day my uncle went to cash his pension cheque and didn't come home. I was alone with my Aunt May. We were so worried about what might have happened because my uncle always came home on time. It was late and I was scared. The next day the State police came to inform us that my uncle had been in a traffic accident and was in hospital. I can't remember how many days or weeks went by before he came home but finally he returned. However, he was not alone; he had a woman with him and she was on crutches. Apparently, she was in the car with him at the time of the accident. Her name was Judy and I didn't like her. She had evil in her eyes and was always drunk.

The two of them would often fight over money or alcohol. Once, they fought over my uncle's tax return form and he pushed her down the stairs, an incident that led to her breaking her leg. While she was living with us my uncle was a totally different person. He stopped caring about the place. All the two of them would do was drink, fight and sleep all day long. My Aunt May was always telling him to take her back where he found her because she was only causing trouble.

She often threatened to kill him and had such an influence on him that he even shot at me for no reason at all. He chased me through the butterbean garden and started shooting. I threw myself on the ground and covered my head, listening to the pellets flying over me. I was so scared that I stayed in the woods until it got dark and then I crawled indoors through the window and into my bed.

I think a major turning point in my life was one evening when I was standing behind a big oak tree watching a bulldozer clearing trees to lay a foundation to build a house. I had never seen a bulldozer so huge. The next evening I was watching it again when suddenly I heard the gentle voice of a woman.

"Hey, young fellow! Come here, you don't have to be scared." She was about five and a half feet in height and had the most beautiful smile I had ever seen. She approached me very slowly, as if I were a strange and lonely animal. "Are you hungry, little fellow? What is your name?" Then she gave me a sandwich. I felt as if the angels had come down from the heavens to rescue me. She had long black hair, with coffee-coloured skin which was very smooth, like that of an Indian. She asked me if I would like to spend a night at her home.

Getting to know her and her family, Will, Mary, Jolen, Joyce, and the Rev. Williams jr, who later adopted me, was the turning point in my life. I was so happy to get away from Uncle Herman that I don't remember even saying goodbye. Because of that lady I am able to sit here and write my life story. My Uncle Herman did not hesitate to sign the necessary documents. Her family became my family, and I praise and thank the Lord for that. Indeed, the Lord does work in mysterious ways.

My father showed up for my first day at school and that was the last time I saw him. Today, I don't know if he is dead or alive. The last time I was home I wanted to visit my mother's grave. But it is no longer there.

THE GROWING YEARS

I was approaching the age of puberty, the time when my sex glands were becoming functional. In short, I was becoming a teenager. My voice began to change, I had skin problems, I was sweating under my arms. Girls were looking at me differently, and I was looking at them in a different way but I was too naive to know what was going on

inside me. So I decided to call this chapter The Growing years.

There I was, spending most of my life in the gutter. I felt like a wild animal. I was living in this strange new world of partially civilised people. The only person who taught me anything about manners and respect was my adopted mother adopted mother. But as for the birds and the bees, girls and the boys, love, all that sort of thing, I had to find out for myself because my brothers weren't around. My stepbrother Will was very religious and he too had no idea but I took it among myself to find out and talked to my stepdad. This man, I should explain, was responsible for my passage into manhood. He was very calm and collected, strict, very loving and caring, a perfect gentlemen. Through him I learnt just about everything that was expected of me in life. He was a preacher who had his own radio show, which was aired every Sunday morning around 10am. Back in the seventies he was also a general contractor and built just about every house in Riverview. As a matter of fact, he built the first Bank of Providence, Forge Virginia, and they appointed him onto their board of trustees but he always had time for the family. I really can't say anything negative about him, mainly because he taught me so much about life and what is really important. He told me about growing up, having respect for older people, and about having proper manners, which the young generation don't appear to have these days. He once told me, "Son, I am depending on you, don't let me down. Can you understand what kind of feeling that gives you to know that someone is depending on you? Sometimes when he gave me a job to do, I would go out of my way to satisfy him. Remember, I was not his child but he never let me know and it was very important for me to be treated equally and be accepted as someone. Today, as a single parent, I too try to teach my boys in the same way, that I was taught, but it's not easy. Today's generation is totally different. Kids today are so influenced by the devil that they don't listen to their parents anymore. I think that if I could turn back time, I would not be in this situation today.

I used to enjoy every minute with my stepfather. He would constantly keeping me laugh and busy. On Saturdays we would get up early and go fishing at West Point, by Ocean view. He had a big boat, so we were able to spend the whole day fishing in the ocean. Around 5pm we would return home with around 30-40 fish, crabs and lobsters. My stepmother would prepare a big skillet with all the right seasoning. Then she would cook them in boiling water over an open fire. I think just about every one from the neighbourhood was there. The one thing I hated was cleaning the fish and crabs. You could wash your hands for hours but the smell of fish was everywhere. When we had finished, me and the boys would get involved in a basketball game. I didn't own my own basketball but my stepbrother Will had one of his own. Unfortunately, he was very stingy. We had to do something for him first, for example wash his car, before he would let us play with his basketball. Sometimes it would last for an hour or two. But most of the time he wasn't home so I would steal his basketball and as soon as we saw his car approaching around the corner, I would sneak it back upstairs in our room. Sometimes, however, he would catch me, because I wasn't quick enough. I got along very well with Martina, Jolen, and Joyce although we had our ups and down like everyone. Martina was the youngest daughter and she was very, very contrary and demanding; you know the type – assertive and determined. When she set her mind on something she would see it through top the end but she was my father's favourite. At this point I should mention I'm tired of saying stepfather, mother, sister and brother, so from now on I shall refer to my father, mother, sister and brother, okay?

Jolen, was very lazy, sometimes too lazy to lift up her feet when she walked. She would prefer to sleep the whole day. You couldn't get her to participate in any kind of activity, she would move along like a turtle. Maybe there was a reason for her apathy but I never got involved, whatever it was. Joyce was a very easy going person, nice and very free spirited. I remember when I went to take my driving test she let me use her car, a yellow Ford Torino, with a long black stripe on each side, like the one Starksy and Hutch used to drive in the TV series. She even let me use her car for my very first prom. Now, let me tell you about my prom. This was the best time of my growing up. The first time I went to the prom was with a beautiful girl, from another school. But what I didn't know was that she was actually my cousin. But that's how it is in the South. Relatives, cousins, sometimes you don't know the difference. I was told that one of my cousins married his own cousin. But anyway, it was a very nice evening together with her. But she had to be home before one o'clock in the morning. Actually, I liked her very much. Later on, she became pregnant by another boy. In 1976, the bi-centennial year, everything was red, white and blue. It was the year I graduated from the High School. Our group, the Panthers, had colours of blue and gold. I also joined the Army that year. Everything was wonderful for me. Just like in the movies, I was a member of the alpha beta club, a top wrestler, good at sports, and so on. I was finally a young man. Eighteen years old. On my own and independent. It's now like history repeating itself as I am here on my own again. But just because I was eighteen I never lost respect for the family that adopted me. I would still think of my adopted mother if I stepped out of line or did something wrong. She used to say "You think because you are eighteen, you are a man, but let me tell you, as long as you are living in this house you still have to do what I say. And I respected that. I remember the first time I got drunk, it was at our graduation party. It was also the very first time I slept away from home. The next day I was so sick, I think, I threw up everywhere. Around three o'clock in the afternoon, I called home. My mother was so angry I was scared to return to her. I knew what would happen. But I still had to go home. Anyway, I made a promise to myself I would never get drunk again. And I kept that promise, even when I was in the military. I didn't drink, smoke, or whatever, until finally the peer pressure got to me. It was in Texas. It seemed so cool to have a cigarette in your hand, and that's how I started smoking. I smoked up until my accident in 1997. I haven't smoked since then.

I often think back to when I was a teenager. I wish I could turn back time. life was treating me good. I had a part-time job at my father's service station, pumping gasoline. I had held a clean driving licence since I was 15 years old. I had girlfriends. What more can you ask for? But I still missed my real mother. Still, I knew she was with me and guiding me all the way. As for my real father... well, that's another chapter. One of the best thing about being a teenager is that your parents, your teacher, and your friends believe they can depend on you. They give you chances, chances to take over different tasks. You are no longer seen as that young and naive little boy or girl and that makes you proud of yourself. But when I look around at the young kids today, I find them lacking responsibility, with no respect for themselves and their environment. Alcohol, drugs and cigarettes are their life. You can see clearly the hate in their eyes; they raise their hands up to their parents. I know what I am talking about because I am going through this with my own boys but I don't believe that the root of the problem is the parents. It depends on their social environment. Community, surrounding and family and friends. Here is an good example. John is 16, his family was separated when he was 7. He lived with his mother in the poorest part of town, his neighbour was well known to the local police. His mother lives off Welfare and he has turned into a little gangster. I think you get the picture. But here in Germany or Russia the problem is that most teenagers, whether they come from a poor or middle-class background, or even a rich family, are heavily influenced by the mass media. new products and trend. Just about every male teenager thinks that he is L.L. Cool-Jay, or wants to be like Eminem; even young girls wants to be like Britney Spears or Pink. Then they want body piercings, tattoos, cosmetic surgery, notably, in the case of girls, silicone breast implants. These are ideas which originated in the United States. And it gets worse. The latest craze, called Jackass, is to do reckless and dangerous things such as jumping out of a 24-floor building or off a cliff. The people who perform these acts want to reach the point of no return. These days, almost every other household has a computer with the internet. Teenagers are becoming more and more influenced by the new technology, mainly because on the internet you can see and find just about anything you want. My boys have reached the stage in their life where they are slowly slipping into that scene. But I constantly warn them of the risks attached to participating in some of the activities that young people now take for granted.

I constantly remind them that God did not create them so that they can see how much pain their body can take, or jump out of trees from great heights without protective gear. I try to teach them that these are acts of evil temptations. But then again, what can i do? They need to find out for themselves otherwise they will never learn.

My Relationships

When it comes to the art of lovemaking, the Arian man is enthusiastic and adventurous. Partners can sometimes be overwhelmed by this spirited approach, something that is not necessarily a sign of their weakness, but simply a reaction to the ardent intensity of passion. The Aries man loves to experiment and to take things to the limit but this Aries lover is writing it all from scratch. It's funny how books know just about everything about an individual. But it's true. The first two sentences are very well written, mainly because it's true. My first relationship as far as I can remember was at the age of 13 but she was 18. It was my very first wet dream. She was my relative but she didn't seem to care and nor did I. It was one of those very hot summer days. She was babysitting my aunt's kids, and was always watching soaps. I happened to be looking for my cousin Roscoe, who was not home. She was always a very active girl. So I guess she took advantage of me. I mean, she had a boyfriend, because she threatened me not to tell anyone. That's why I will omit her name and details. But it was so good we would do it as often as possible. We did it at my aunt's house and once at our house, even in my parents' bed. Then I fell in love with her. I know it was only puppy love but at the time it was real for me. I mean, I was still a kid. In school, holding hands and kissing behind the school walls was normal. Once I was discovered kissing my girlfriend behind the school walls. The principal, Mr L.McMann, caught us in the act. He threatened to tell my father, but I knew that if he told my father he would have just laughed. I mean, it wasn't as though we'd broken a law or something. It was the last days of school before the summer break. One thing I haven't mentioned is that I always thought that I was ugly, and no one was interested in me. But that proved to be wrong. In High School I had at least three girlfriends at the same time. Mind you, it isn't easy to maintain three relationships. I would break up with one as soon as I met another. I know it's not fair but again, nature has proven to me that I am handsome. And slowly I begin to like going to school. I think during the later days of my education I missed maybe 4 days from school. Later own, as I was growing up, my body began to change. And as I got older I began to look for relationships more in my own age. But not all of the time. For example, older women prefer young men and or older men seek younger women. There are thousands of reasons why but I it didn't apply in my case. I wasn't bothered as long as my partner was a woman. Like, for example, my cousin, the one I mentioned earlier. By law, this would have been statutory rape because of the fact was that I was only 13 years old. Again, I recall once a young girl around 12 was in love with me and I was 19. When I came to Germany I felt as if I was in 'Hog Heaven'! I felt like a king. The European women liked the American GIs especially the blacks; it was awesome. My sister's husband Michael told me that if I ever decide to joined the Army, ask to be stationed in Germany. He said it is extreme cold in Germany but the women there are beautiful; and you know what? He was right. Here, the ratio is 2:1 and in simple English that means there are twice as many women than men. Although it's true, they don't have a baby boom as in China and Japan. I came to Germany in the middle of December 1977. I think the first time I stepped outside of the base where I was stationed was in January 1978. First, I could not speak the language, count their money and had no ideal of how to make contact with them. But in the spring, I would take my camera, go to the city park and take pictures of everybody and everything I could see. Later on, I was in McDonalds, and there I met a young girl who spoke perfect English. I thought she was American. We dated each other and later fell in love, but eventually we began to have problems because I found out that she knew just about everyone in the whole base. I had good reason to be jealous, but she was more jealous of me. I wanted to break up with her so many times, but it was hard, she would threaten to kill herself and sometimes she tried. Two years later, I finally broke up with her. I will never forget that ordeal. Incidentally, she was my first German girlfriend. After her, I met many other women and fell in love many times. I think in the last 15-20 years here, I had maybe 10 relationships that lasted over 6 months; there were a couple that lasted over two months. I do not want to go into the details of each and every relationship but I am going to mention some of the major factors that caused much damage to my life, otherwise this book would be incomplete.

In 1995 I met an Eastern European women, her name was Vivian. Vivian was very pretty with typically Slovakian features, a round face, and cat-like eyes. And she had only one thing in mind – sex. I met her in one of the local bars, where I would constantly hang out. The owner was a Greek women name Eve, I knew she was married but for some reason it didn't matter to her. After the first two dates we fell in love. Not long afterwards, she mentioned to me that she had a little girl name Marietta, and we soon got to meet each other. Without any hesitation, they both moved in with my boys and me. In the beginning we were having a lot of conflicts, mainly because my kids didn't like them interfering in our lives shortly afterwards she became pregnant with my son Bobby, who is now seven years old. I think the nine months of the pregnancy were the worst time of my life. After the birth of Bobby, I wanted only to get away from her. I offered to take Bobby with me, but she wasn't interested. I finally decided to move into a three-bedroomed flat with my two boys.

But she came along just about every day and night. I helped her to get her own flat but because she did not pay the rent she was kicked out. And because I could not bear the thought of my baby being out on the streets, I took them in. We then moved to another town, and there my life began to go down the drain. My kids did not like the school there and my boss refused to pay me my money. Anyway, in order to feed my family, I had to turn to the welfare office. And the amount of tension that was being caused finally resulted in my accident. In 1999, after I was released from the rehabilitation centre, and because the flat where we were living was so small for my new situation, I moved back to the town where I was station, when I was in the Military. Into a was something of a skyscraper. There, Vivian started to use my handicap to her advantage. What I mean is that she would often leave me alone the whole day without anything to eat or drink. Once she left me the whole night alone. Then she would steal large amounts of my money to have a drug party. I pressed charges against her and she did the same against me. We each received a punishment of three years probation. I was foolish because she persuaded me to buy her a computer so that she could search for a job. Instead, however, she searched for a man and found one. All of a sudden she wanted to move out and get married to the man she met on the Internet. He was a White American, from West Virginia. I think he flew back and forth at least three times in one year to be with her. When he was not here, she and her prostitute girlfriend were having the time of their life. Then she met another (Black) American in a local disco and she told me she had broken up with the other one for no reason at all. Now she has another four-month-old baby from her new boyfriend, whom she is yet to marry. Today I am having constantly difficulties with her as she is trying to deny me all contact between me and my little boy. So you see, for some reason I always seem to end up meeting the wrong women.

I have had a relationship with a woman since I sustained my handicap but it lasted just six weeks. She was pretty, I'd known her since she was 13 and by then she was 38 years old. If you were to see her figure and looks you'd probably take her for around guess she is 25. She was the first woman that accepted my handicap. She would treat me as if I was normal. I would have loved to have had a sexual relationship with her because I found her attractive. But then again, where there's good, there is also bad. She was a woman that quickly fell in love with men. And she would get pregnant too hastily. She has three children from three different fathers. I heard that the last relationship didn't last too long. She loved to argue with me. We would have a normal discussion and it would often end in an argument. You see, she always wanted to be in the right and I do not give in that easily either. Most of the arguments were because of the kids and she convinced herself that all men are dumb and wanted only one thing. It was too much for me so I summoned up the will free myself from her. I still see her occasionally passing by on her bike, but that's about it. I had another relationship with a woman named Christine, whom I met through a friend. We went together for about a year until I found out she was a criminal and on the run from the law. I also discovered she was a liar and thief. She had been living in California for seven years and was married with two boys. Her husband was a Hispanic. And if all that wasn't enough she was working in the home entertainment department,of a shopping mall, confiscating video players and selling them. She was finally caught and given a custodial sentence. However, she kidnapped her children and was caught trying to board a plane to Germany. Her husband took the children and told her to go back to Germany otherwise she would have to go to jail. Here, I helped her to find employment at a cleaning company and there she had a job as a driver, driving and picking up women from different cleaning jobs. Once she was stopped for speeding and she did not had a valid driving licence. Later, we moved away from the city to live in the country, in a five-bedroomed house, because she was hoping that her children could come to Germany and live with us. Again, I helped her to find employment at a local supermarket and there she worked in the meat section. She had to work until closing time and was always the last one to lock up the store. Then she began to do what she did best. But eventually she was caught and given two choices: she must quit, or the store would press charges against her. Then later I broke up with her because of her lying and because she was dating another man behind my back.

So you see, I have had my share of different types of relationships. Today, I am single and hoping that my soul mate is out there somewhere.

AN ORDEAL

*W*hat is an ordeal? you may ask. What is the meaning of an ordeal? Ok, let's talk about it a little. Maybe we can define it as being 'a severe or trying experience'. As long ago as I can remember, it was always some kind of setback or one of those 'ups and downs' in my life. This belief started back in my childhood, after my mother died. That was the biggest ordeal for me back then and still it haunts me to this day.

Now I am a grown man. Everything I know is down to myself and the guidance of the Lord, my saviour and my healer. Other than my three boys, he is the only friend and helper that I have ever had. I am prepared to meet my Maker. Whether my Maker is prepared for the great ordeal of meeting me is another matter.

One ordeal began when I joined the Army because the man who persuaded me to join the Army lied to me. He promised me that Booth Camp would be easy, and after six weeks of basic training everything would be simple and straightforward. But it was a lie. A big lie. It was in Texas, a military camp called McGregory Range, around the middle of August, about106F, and somewhere in the hot desert by the road. It was so bad that the water in my container was too hot to drink. Some of the trainees were passing out owing to dehydration; some of them, me included, were seeing mirages. it was a real ordeal. I began to think I was in hell. The only thing I wanted was to get away from the Army. I was not cut out for this way of life. The Army had brainwashed us to the point that everything we should think of must be military and our country. America was the greatest country in the whole universe. The pressure was so strong that I planned my own death. Yes, that's right, I had all the details on how I was going to carry it out. You see, we had to pull gaurd duty. We had to gaurd the ammo bunker, the motor pool, etc. I had a M16 rife, which can be put on full automatic and I had live rounds. It was easy to do but something changed me in the middle of my military career. It was a woman, yes, a woman. She was 5'4, with long black hair, and hazel brown eyes. She was a beautiful young Mexican woman. Her name was Chavella. This woman changed the course of my life. I was so much in love that I no longer thought of taking my life. She gave me the affection, love and caring that I was lacking.

Such feelings of depression often happen in a person's life, especially in the case of older people or people that have lost a love one in the war, or some kind of sickness. Most ordeals happen in situations similar to the one I endured when I was stationed here in Germany in 1977. I was often depressed because it wasn't like America here. You were a guest in a strange country; their customs and way of life were not what you were used to. The language and culture barriers were such a problem. Anyway, there was that one time when I was once so down and depressed that i wanted to take my life. But this time it was different from being back in Texas. The plot and the ideal were the same. It was like this: at 5pm I intended to patrol the motorpool where they kept all the military vehicles, jeeps, tanks, etc. My plan was to shoot myself. At 4pm, one hour prior to going on duty, I had to report to the Armoury to pick up my weapon and ammunitions. As I was walking towards the weapons depot I happened to pass the post chaplin. It was if the Lord had sent him in my direction. He stopped me and began to talk to me. The next thing I knew he was giving me reasons as to why I should not take my life. He said to me, "If you can't make it in the military," my son, "well then you can't make it anywhere in life." I remember those words over and over again. And after that talk with the chaplin I felt like a new man. I had a new reason to live.

The years went by and everytime I was in a situation where I didn't know what to do or which direction to go I would pray to the Lord and ask him to guide me and he always did so. My traffic accident in 1997 was the biggest ordeal of my life. I had been in traffic accidents before, but they only resulted in minor injuries. This time, however, it was devastating. I was once held at gunpoint by the police for more than one hour because me and my friends were mistaken for someone else. The police were sure that we had kidnapped a German woman with the intention of raping her. They finally realised that we were not the ones they were looking for. Over the years I, and deep down I'm pretty sure you too, have had some kind of an ordeal which you have lived through. Remember, an ordeal is not something that is planned. It's something that just happens.

My stay in Germany

B efore I begin I'd like to share with you some information about Germany and the German people. Germany has a population of approximately 82.1 million (including 7.3 million foreigners) and is one of the most densely populated countries in all of Europe with 230 people per square kilometre. Only Belgium, the Netherlands and Great Britain have a higher population density.

The population is distributed very unevenly. The Berlin region has been growing rapidly since Germany's unification and presently has more than 4.3 million inhabitants. More than 11 million people (about 1,100 per square kilometre) live in the Rhine-Ruhr industrial region, where towns and cities are so close together that there are no distinct boundaries between them.

Other concentrations are to be found in the Rhine-Main area around Frankfurt, Wiesbaden and Mainz, the Rhine-Neckar industrial region around Mannheim and Ludwigshafen, the industrial area around Stuttgart, and the catchment areas of Bremen, Cologne, Dresden, Hamburg, Leipzig, Munich and Nuremberg/Furth.

These densely populated regions contrast markedly with thinly populated areas such as the heathlands and moorlands of the North

German Plain, parts of the Eifel Mountains, the Bavarian Forest, the Upper Palatinate, the March of Brandenburg and large parts of Mecklenburg-Western Pomerania.

The western part of Germany is much more densely populated than the eastern part, where less than one fifth of the population (15.3 million) live on roughly 30 percent of the national territory. Of the 20 cities with more than 300,000 inhabitants, three are in the eastern part of Germany.

Nearly one third of the population (about 25 million people) live in the 82 large cities with more than 100,000 inhabitants. But the majority of people in the Federal Republic live in small towns and villages: nearly 6.4 million in municipalities with a population of fewer than 2,000 and 50.5 million in towns with between 2,000 and 100,000 inhabitants.

The population of the old and new states began to decline in the 1970s because the birth-rate was falling. Germany had one of the lowest birth-rates in the world in the year 1998: 10.2 births per 1,000 inhabitants per year (in the western part of the country). The population increase after the Second World War was due mainly to immigration. Some 13 million refugees and expellees entered the present German territory from the former German eastern provinces and Eastern Europe.

There was a continuous flow of people fleeing from Eastern to Western Germany until the Berlin Wall was erected by the regime in the former German Democratic Republic (GDR) in 1961, which hermetically sealed the border. Beginning in the early 1960s, large numbers of foreign workers came to the Federal Republic of old whose expanding economy needed additional labour which was not available at home.

Regional disparities

The German nation essentially grew out of a number of German tribes, e.g. the Franks, the Saxons, the Swabians and the Bavarians. These old tribes have, of course, long since lost their original character, but their traditions and dialects live on in their respective regions. Those ethnic regions are not, however, identical to the present states (Lander), most of which were only formed after the Second World War in agreement with the occupying powers. In many cases the boundaries were drawn without any consideration for old traditions. Furthermore, the flow of refugees and the massive post-war migrations, along with the mobility of the modern industrial society, have more or less blurred the ethnic boundaries.

Since time immemorial, different characteristics have been ascribed to the various regional groups. Natives of Mecklenburg, for instance, are considered reserved, Swabians thrifty, Rhinelanders happy-go-lucky, and Saxons hardworking and shrewd – traditional observations that are gladly perpetuated to this day in a spirit of good-natured folkloric rivalry.

The German language

German is one of a large group of Indo-Germanic languages, and within that category one of the Germanic languages. It is thus related not only to Danish, Norwegian, Swedish, Dutch and Flemish, but also to English. The emergence of a common High German language is attributed to Martin Luther's translation of the Bible.

Germany has a wealth of dialects. It is usually possible to determine a German's native region from his or her dialect and pronunciation. These dialects differ greatly: if, for instance, a Mecklenburger and a Bavarian or a Baden-Württemberg native were to carry on a conversation in their respective pure dialects, they would have great difficulty in understanding each other.

German is also the native language in Austria, Liechtenstein, most of Switzerland, South Tirol (northern Italy), northern Schleswig (Denmark) and in small areas of Belgium, France (Alsace) and Luxembourg along the German border. The German minorities in Poland, Romania and the countries of the former Soviet Union have also partly retained the German language.

German is the native language of more than 100 million people. About one in ten books published throughout the world is originally written in German. As regards translations into foreign languages, German is third after English and French, and more works have been translated into German than into any other language.

National minorities

Germany has signed the European Council's Skeleton Agreement for the Protection of National Minorities for the four national minorities residing in Germany from early times: the Sorbs, Frisians, Danes and the German Sinti and Roma peoples. It has also signed for the European Charter for Regional or Minority Languages. The agreement of 1998 has now become incorporated into German law.

The Lusatian Sorbs are the descendants of Slavic tribes. They settled in the territory east of the Elbe and Saale rivers in the 6th century during the migration of peoples that occurred in the early centuries A.D. The first document in which they are mentioned is dated 631. In the 16th century, under the influence of the Reformation, a written Sorbian language evolved. In addition to the Institute for Sorbian Studies at the University of Leipzig, there are a large number of schools, associations and other institutions which are devoted to the cultivation of the Sorbian language and culture.

The Frisians are the descendants of a Germanic tribe on the North Sea coast (between the Lower Rhine and the Ems River) and have preserved numerous traditions in addition to their own distinctive language. A

Danish minority lives in the Schleswig region of the state of Schleswig-Holstein, especially around Flensburg.

The number of Sinti and Roma peoples with German citizenship is estimated at 70,000. The Central Council for German Sinti and Roma, which has received support from the German government since 1982, gives strong voice to the compensation of holocaust survivors, minority rights and the preservation of the Romani language while tackling discrimination and prejudice.

Foreign nationalities

Of the country's approximately 82.1 million inhabitants (1998), 7.3 million are foreigners. They were all glad to come and stay in Germany (see table, p. 499). For decades there were no racial problems. The category of 'guest workers', initially consisting of Italians, was extended to include Greeks and Spaniards, and then Portuguese, Yugoslavs and Turks.

Integration within the European Union and the Western world, the dissolution of the Eastern bloc, and the immigration of people from Asian and African countries naturally meant a considerable increase in the number of foreigners of diverse origin having come to live in Germany.

The Federal Republic has proved itself to be an open society not only by taking in asylum-seekers and war refugees. It has also always been a champion of the free movement of labour, freedom of occupation and freedom of establishment within the European Union. Approximately 2.7 million German repatriates from the countries of the former Eastern bloc, especially from the territory of the former Soviet Union, have come to the Federal Republic of Germany since 1987; in 1999 they numbered more than 104,916.

Germany's willingness to open its doors to foreigners who have been persecuted on political grounds is unparalleled. The new Article 16a of the Basic Law, like the former Article 16, still guarantees protection from political persecution as an individual basic right. In 1989 the number of foreigners seeking asylum in Germany was 121,318; in 1991 the figure rose to 256,112 and in 1992 to 438,191. At the same time, the proportion of those who could be recognised as genuine victims of political persecution fell to less than five percent. In 1993 some 322,600 asylum-seekers entered Germany. Their number fell significantly when the new legislation on the right of asylum became effective on 1 July 1993: Only 127,210 people sought asylum in 1994; 127,937 in 1995; 116,367 in 1996; 104,353 in 1997; 98,644 in 1998; and 95,113 in 1999. Under the new constitutional amendment, which has been in force since 1 July 1993 (the so-called asylum compromise), the right of asylum has been focused on its true purpose – the normal state of affairs in other countries – of affording protection to those who have actually been persecuted on political grounds and really do need protection. As a result, foreigners who enter Germany from a safe third country may no longer invoke this basic right. Germany also reserves the right, notwithstanding the Geneva Convention relating to the status of refugees, to draw up a list of countries where, according to official sources of information, no one is subject to persecution so that there is, as a rule, no grounds for asylum. Nonetheless, anyone whose application for asylum has been rejected may appeal, if necessary, right through to the Federal Constitutional Court.

Policy on foreigners and naturalisation

More than half of the foreigners residing in Germany have lived here for at least ten years; almost one third of them have lived here for 20 years or more. Of the foreigners who have resided here for at least ten years, about 870,000 are under the age of 25. More than two thirds of the children and adolescents were born here.

On 1 January 2000, important regulations contained in the new law reforming citizenship came into effect. The essential aspects are that in accordance with the law, children born in Germany to foreign parents now receive German citizenship at birth. The prerequisite is that Germany has been the usual legal residence of one parent for the previous eight years and that this parent possesses a residence certificate or has had an unlimited residence permit for the previous three years. When, by virtue of parentage, these children acquire another citizenship, they must choose between German and foreign citizenship upon reaching maturity at the age of 18.

- The law grants a special limited right of citizenship under the same conditions to children who have not reached the age of 10 as from 1 January 2000.
- Foreigners may now claim citizenship after eight years (previously 15 years). This claim is dependent on a sufficient command of the German language and acceptance and knowledge of the German constitution. Citizenship for foreign political extremists is excluded by way of a new protective clause. Fundamentally, in order to acquire citizenship, one's previous nationality must be forfeited; exceptions are determined according to law.
- When an individual applies for and acquires foreign citizenship, he or she automatically forfeits German citizenship, regardless of whether or not he or she continues to reside within Germany.
- At the same time, the opportunity to retain German citizenship in such cases of automatic loss has been extended by means of authorisation of such retention.
- Emigrants of German origin from Eastern European states are automatically naturalised upon issuance of an appurtenant certificate confirming their special status or presentation of a

late repatriate certificate. The separate naturalisation process hitherto in place is no longer valid.

The interests of foreigners living in Germany are represented by the Federal Government's Commissioner for Matters relating to Aliens. The Commissioner is concerned with the conception of and individual issues pertaining to policy on foreigners and to this end conducts talks with German and foreign politicians, representatives of the parties to collective bargaining agreements, and other groups within society. In particular, this is the person approached by organisations actively involved in matters pertaining to foreigners. Above all, the Commissioner supports initiatives to promote the interests of foreigners permanently residing in Germany. For this reason, the Commissioner is also constantly in contact with the embassies of the countries in which Germany formerly recruited labour and visits these countries and meets with government representatives there to discuss pertinent issues.

One important task of the Commissioner is to disseminate comprehensive and factual information on the history of employment of foreigners in Germany and its economic significance, the origination and development of German policy on foreigners, humanitarian aspects of the actual immigration situation for foreigners and Germans alike, and the political and legal obligations assumed by Germany under international conventions and declarations.

My personal experience with German peoples is as followed. I am a person who gets along with everybody. It does not matter if you are German or belongs to other minority groups. When I look at German people today – mainly young people – I feel the American way of life has influence the people, young population is so strong that I sometimes begin to think "Am I in American. American TV programs, movies, fashion, fast food, etc. And English is being spoken more and more. Compared to the time when

I first arrived in Germany. Today, it seems as though every second word is English. Every teenager wears American products. Or whatever the trend is. My stay here was sometimes rewarding and, many of the time depressing. I learnt that German people are very stereotype and courageless. If you want to sell them a product, I wish you a lot of luck trying to convince them. They expect a guarantee, and needs a day or two to think about it.

The criminal law system is similar to that of Mexico, there is much corruption. The administration system is very confusing, because you have to apply for just about everything and you can be waiting for up to a year before you get a reply. I don't agree with the penalty law because if you are stopped by law enforcement agents, i.e. the police, you do not have any rights. You will be charged on the grounds of suspicion. Sadly to say, but foreigners suffers the most. Believe me; I have had my ups and downs with the justice system here. Over the last twenty years, my life here has changed. The cost of living here is very expensive. In the present moment, Germany has over 5.3% (May 2013) million unemployed. Germany has a well-developed social security system. As a jobholder paying statutory social security payments, you are sure of being protected against the biggest risks – for example illness, occupational accidents, unemployment, or when you grow old. Here, we explain about the different types of statutory social security that exist and what the situation is regarding your entitlements if you want to move back to your home country. But the welfare system takes care of unemployment and no-one has to accept a job if they don't like it.

However, I do not have any problem with the people here. Some are warm-hearted, many are cold hearted and bold. I have experience both at work and in social life. Such as my private assistant Veronica or my very good friend, Frank, who I have worked with. After I finished the military here I decided to stay on because I had a good paying job offer working in my profession, photographer.

I remember my very first job here at one of Germany largest photo laboratory (Foto-Park. I never understood how can they hire someone who could not speak the language – apart from *JA* and *nein*. When a question was asked I would always reply with JA. Slowly began to learn the language; I think it took me about three years. But even today I can't speak it or write it perfectly. But it doesn't bother me because according to a survey here, over 500 thousand people in Germany cannot read or write.

As in all jobs everybody wants to be the boss. I've had good and bad experience in some job here. In fact, considering I was a foreigner with little knowledge of the culture and the language. I had worked in Administration office of the city mayor's office at the City Hall. There, I had the opportunity to learn about the law system. Having working at University (as photographer for a scientist, was very interesting, learning about human genetics. And working as a camera man at the only TV studio in the city where I am residing was also exciting and educational.

Since my stay I here, I've also had the chance to visit other surrounding countries such as Austria, Paris, England, Spain,Turkey,Czech Republic and Switssland. I still have not made it to Italy, but if the lord prevails it, then I will.

THE MARRIAGE

*I*n 1984 I decided, or maybe I should say I was forced, to get married to a young German woman. Her name was Jennifer. We had two kids, Harold and Michael. Today, Harold is 20 and Michael, who lives with me, is 17 and currently in the middle of his apprenticeship in woodwork. Harold lives and studies in Wurzberg, Germany. He too is serving an apprenticeship, in agriculture.

I didn't want to get married but was forced into it owing to a crazy custom. My wife was under a lot of pressure from her family to marry because here in Germany the custom is that if you have a child and are not married then the child is considered to be illegitimate. So, very reluctantly, I played along with it. The marriage was a simple one. It took place at the City Hall and was certainly not a religious ceremony. We did not have a ring bearer or a flower girl, but a good reception party was held.

The main reason I didn't want to get married was my fear that I might one day be faced with divorce. Ironically, six years later that's exactly what happened. Not because I wanted too, but because I had no alternative.

Now before I tell you what happened, maybe you would like to go to the toilet or maybe get some refreshments as this is a long story. Nevertheless, it is a story worth telling. I think I mentioned I was a disc jockey in a disco in Erlanger, Germany. It started like this. I was working in a military base, where I was once stationed, in the snack bar as a cook. A friend approached me and offered me a part-time job as a disc jockey in a local dance club called Sugar Shake. I had never performed for German people. As a matter of fact, back then I could not speak German but it didn't really matter. The only thing that matters is that I performed well and they all liked me. I was the very first black American disc jockey in the city. Loads of people came from all over to listen to me. I was in the local newspaper and on TV. On Friday and Saturday nights, the disco would be completely packed. I had become a public figure, and was nicknamed 'Super jock'. I was popular with both the young and old. I didn't have any problem with women. Because I was a popular disc jockey, the girls were crazy about me. In fact, that is how I met my wife. She was the one I had been waiting for; I was tired of one night stands and wanted to finally settle down and maybe start a family. Anyway, she was very pretty, blond, with baby blue eyes; there was something about her and I knew I had to get to know her. She used to come every Saturday night and we would always make eye contact. Then one night I decided to buy her a drink. At first, she didn't want to accept my drink but as the weeks passed I got to know her better (or so I thought). Our first night together led to six years of marriage and finally she became pregnant with my oldest son. That was in 1982. Three years later in 1985 my second son Michael was born. At that time I really thought I had the perfect and everlasting marriage. I had a good job, I was earning good money and had a wife that loved me. I also had two beautiful sons. It felt as though nothing could go wrong. I had given up playing music and had found a good job making good money. However, as in every marriage, there were difficulties. There are good days and bad days and you inevitably have disagreements from time to time. It didn't take long to realise that my wife was very jealous. Don't get me wrong. I too can be jealous but not that jealous. She was suspicious of everything and everybody. I suspect that somewhere in her past she had been disappointed and left feeling wounded because of an encounter or relationship with another man. Indeed, she told me once about a man she had been deeply in love with. She was even pregnant by him but the babies were born as Siamese twins and their lives were terminated. Anyway, her boyfriend treated her very badly, even during her pregnancy. I wasn't aware of these things until well into our marriage. In addition to her feelings of jealousy she was very sensitive. Sometimes I had to watch what I said to her. She took jokes very seriously. I think the break-up of our marriage came soon after my son Harold was born. because during her pregnancy she gained a lot of weight. I used to tell her not to keep eating all kinds of junk food. Don't get me wrong, I know it's normal for a woman to eat in that way during pregnancy. However, in my wife's case it was extreme. Then one day I came home from work in a bad mood because I had had a stressful day at work. We were eating dinner but somehow she was eating like a pig. It was so bad that I couldn't enjoy my meal. So I told her she looked and ate like a pig. By saying such things, our marriage began to change. She took it so serious and then after I realised what I had said I apologised to her but somehow it just didn't work; the damage had been done. I tried telling her it didn't matter if she was skinny or fat, I loved her the way she was. I often said those words to her but somehow she just blocked out everything I said. She tried all kinds of diet plans and I gave her lots of money to help her with them. However, I guess it was not enough. She wanted to prove to herself she was still attractive. That is when my best friend, Henry, stepped into the picture. I was too blind and stupid to realise what was gone on around me. I guess I was too busy with work and the kids.

Now let me tell you a bit about my best friend BJ. He came from New York and was base here in the Army. I met him through a close friend of mine. Her name was Sonja and at the time he was seeing her. However, in 1978 he went back to America. He left Sonja with their son Jayjay, who I use to babysit from time to time. Sonja was very heavy build, but had a good sense of humour.

Anyway, one night my wife and I were having one of our daily arguments, and I decided to move out. I jumped in my car and went to Connie's house, because I knew that BJ was there. I explained the problem that I was having with my wife. BJ immediately got dressed, and we both went into the city to a bar. Around ten o' clock BJ said we had to go home because he was working the next day. Nevertheless, I stayed. Around one o' clock in the morning I decided to go back home.

I arrived shortly afterwards and as I approached, I noticed that BJ's car was in my parking place. I began to wonder what was going on. But I soon realised. After I had questioned my wife, she admitted that BJ often came to the house eating and drinking coffee while I was at work. What's more, she claimed, BJ gave her something that was missing when she was with me. He made her feel like a woman again. He accepted her the way she was. For me, well, it was the biggest shock of my life. I couldn't believe this was happening to me. I asked myself over and over again what I had done wrong. I didn't go out with other women, I was not committing adultery, and I really believed that my marriage was perfect. I thought I must be dreaming. However, I was not dreaming, it was really happening. So to cut a long story short I decided to move out. I move to a friend's who was having the same problem with his wife. His name was Jack and we used to work together. After being away from my family for several weeks, it was over as far as I was concerned. I had caught my friend and my wife together and that was the end of it. The only thing that was important to me was my children. Or so it seemed...

My wife continued to call me and would even try to speak to me when I was at work. She would plead to me to come back home. Eventually I relented and did so.

My marriage went well for more than two years and we managed to put the BJ affair behind us. In fact, he was sent back to America. Two years later, however, my wife made contact with a young woman called Mary. Mary was a single parent with two children, a boy and a girl. My wife would frequently go to Mary's house to study the Bible. Mary was a Jehovah witness, a sect which I personally disapprove of. They believe they are perfect people. I did not and do not believe that, because no one is perfect. One day, my wife asked me if she could go out to dinner with Mary. I told her that I didn't mind in the least. Why should I have done? However, the next my dear wife didn't come home and the kids and I were worried that something had happened to her. I waited until around noon then began to make telephone calls, without success. Next I decided to go to Mary's house, which was about three blocks away. As I approach her home, I notice there was an American car parked outside, and I knew there were no Americans living in the area, other than me, and a couple others. I rang her doorbell, she lived on the fifth floor; suddenly, she opened her bathroom window and looked down to see who was there then closed it again. I immediately became suspicious. The door opened and I raced in. I begin knocking on her door frantically. "Where is my wife!" I shouted.

She shouted back at me, "Look, I do not want to have anything to do with it!" I was so full of anger that I pushed my way inside. In the living room, there was my wife. On the table was a pack of cigarettes and in the ashtray was a cigarette, which was still burning. Then suddenly he appeared. I could not I believe my eyes. He was about five feet ten inches, and as black as the night.

"What's up, brother?" Can you imagine how I felt at that moment? For a start, he was not my brother, and I felt like killing them all. But I remained cool. I calmly suggested to her that we go home without any fuss. You know, this time it didn't bother me as much as the first time. I now realised that the women I married wasn't satisfied with one man, she was constantly looking for new adventures.

Once again I moved out of our apartment but it wasn't easy because of the children. A good friend gave me a tip. "Jamie," he said, "this time when you go, do not look back." Today, I can say he was right. I did not look back and my life is beginning to move forward. I was only able to have my boys every second weekend but, surprisingly, she and I became good friends. She would often come by when her lover was working or on duty, and we would drink a bottle of wine or whatever. My kids would sometimes sneak over to my place but she never found out about it. Therefore, you can see how much she was taking care of them. Between my apartment and hers was a big intersection, where traffic crossed in four directions. In addition, back then, Harold was seven and Michael was three. Yet they would both cross the intersection to come to me.

As for their mother, she was not happy with her lover. I saw him one day with another woman in his car. I told her about it and she mentioned it to him but he swore to her she was just a friend. Then the shocking news came.

One weekend, my son Harold mentioned to me that his mother was planning to go to America and most likely I would not see them anymore. Nevertheless, I did not believe him. I told him it is not true, and that we would always stay together. As it happened it turned out to be true but she was very clever about her intentions. First, she told the youth service (social services), that I was constantly interrupting her life, by calling or dropping in. They warned me to keep away from her. This was the other part of her plan, to escape without me knowing about it. I found out later that she had left one week ago for America taking both kids with her. Because I was calling and the phone was always busy, I think I almost had a nerves breakdown. Her mother and father knew about her plans. I immediately contacted my lawyer but it was too late; the police reported that she was already in America. I felt depressed because if I had taken my son seriously, maybe I could have prevented doing what she did. Here's a word of advice to parents: take your children serious, when they are trying to tell you something. The thought that my children were somewhere in the USA, a strange country that they were not used to, was slowly killing me slowly. In addition, my wife had no idea what to expect. After two months of praying, the Lord heard my prayer. My lawyer called me to let me know that her lawyer had been in touch and the kids were doing fine. They were living somewhere in Texas, in a trailer park, which was inhabited solely by black people. Except for her, of course. She was the only white women in the whole neighbourhood and I can imagine what went on there. My son told me he often felt lonely and depressed because he could not speak any English. The other kids would tease him and even beat him. He once told me a boy who was much bigger than he was began to beat him up in front of the house. His girlfriend was watching from the living room window and laughing. My son had no future there. He was very unhappy and wanted to come home, back to the place and the environment he knew. After months of negotiating with her lawyer, the judge was not satisfied because her lawyer insisted we should leave her in America. The kids were fine and she had found the man of her life. Anyway, the judge gave her three weeks to return to Germany with both kids, otherwise he would contact INTERPOL. After almost two months, she returned to Germany with the kids. She wanted to get a quick divorce so she could get married again to her new lover. The children were appointed to me, at that time Michael was four and Harold was seven years old. As promised she returned to America. We then lost contact with her for more than three years. The kids were doing well in school and kindergarten. My dream had come true, I had my two boys back, and we were one happy family again. We moved out of my one-room flat and back to our old three-roomed one. In addition, we remoulded the flat to bury all old memories. I was working at the University as a scientific photographer, hoping to become a professor. Being a single parent meant everything to me. I knew that I would have to make choices and decisions. I lost some friends because I was not able to go out to bars or discos or parties but it didn't bother me at all. My boys were the main thing in my life. I would cry at night with joy and happiness and hold them both in my arms as they slept. Sometimes the three of us would cry together. I felt a sense of obligation, and I had to fulfill these obligations because they were my flesh and blood. I was always there for them. Through good times and through bad times, or when they were ill, I was there, with no help from anyone accept my God. He led me on until they were old enough to look after themselves.

Now, just when you think things are going well, the Devil always tries to change things for the worse. In many cases, he succeeds. In my case, my ex-wife, after three years, suddenly showed up in Germany, and began to make my life and it was the same for the kids. Here I was again, in and out of court because she didn't seem to know where she belonged. It began to take away my energy. You see, the kids – especially Harold – did not want to see her at all and Michael agreed with pretty much everything Harold said. For example, the judge asked them whether he wanted to live with his father or his mother. Harold answered "my father" and Michael did too. But the situation was not clear cut or pleasant for the children. They were torn apart by this separation. Michael did not recognise his mother. Finally, we were divorced. For me it was no cause for celebration. She decided to go back to America but shortly afterwards returned to Germany yet again because living in America was too much for her. Her husband locked her in the house and gave her no money. She was allowed to eat little more than peanut butter and sardines and he would often beat her up. Her husband dated his ex-wife, and she discovered he had another child, also in America. Finally, she was raped on a billiard table by his brother in a country bar back in Kentucky, and everyone was watching, even his mother. The Sheriff was called but because she was so drunk, there was nothing that the law could do. They suggested she go back to Germany so she sold everything that she owned to buy a ticket. Then later we both became friends, just for the sake of the children. She had her own flat somewhere in a small village. I allowed the kids to spend as much time with her as they wanted because to be honest I was glad of the break. Nevertheless, Harold did not want to go to her and it wasn't easy trying to persuade him to. However, after some time he agreed to see her. My life during this time wasn't easy. It was a day-to-day struggle. When I think about, I dedicated half of my life raising them both. Their mother had the time of her life, dating one man after another and in doing so hoping to find someone she could live off. As it worked out, she did, and it happened to be a friend of mine (again). If you have been following this chapter, you will notice that each man my ex-wife went with was a friend of mine. Therefore, you can work out for yourself what kind of person she is. She had heard about the New Year's Eve party I was planning, and called me because she had no plans of her own and that she would be alone (another one of her tricks). So being the nice guy I am, I invited her to come over. She came along and there she met my friend Joe" Let me explain a little about Joe. He was also from Virginia, and was well educated. He was a cook in the Army, but now sells insurance. We became close friends. He helped me out of a few tight corners and I like to think I helped him too. When we went out together, I would agree to be the driver because he liked a drink or two. When I found out that my wife had run off to America with the kids, he was there for me to help me with the ordeal. However, as with all insurance agents, they had their way of manipulating a person to achieve their own objectives, which in this case was money. That was how he was. Always thinking business, money and how to make more money. He did not have a girlfriend. The only women that he knew were through me, or through other friends. However, I liked him because he was funny with his deep south accent. I once built a bar for him in his apartment and it became a popular 'You-drop-inn'. Anyway, he knew my wife but she didn't like him because she thought he was like all my friends, only wanting to go out with me in order to meet other women, which was not true. Anyway, at the party they became very close to each other; so close, in fact, that she eventually married him. It was her third marriage inside just five years. It didn't bother me that they were together; my only concern was that the kids were not involved as my son Harold always looked upon him as Uncle Joe. She finally had someone she had control over and to this day she still has control over him and his wallet. Our friendship broke up because of her. As a matter of fact he broke off all contact with his friends to make her happy. I don't know why, but we are now enemies. Still, I really don't care because these days just one of us is happy and it's certainly not him. However, I should warn him. Today she is a Jehovah witness, and thinks that she is living a perfect life. On Sunday she goes to church and acts as if she is so religious but after church she goes back to her wicked ways. And she has the nerve to go from house to house! But I learnt from the Bible that you should turn away anyone who knocks on your door and says they are the real God. She is now aged 47 and still thinks she's 20 and that's because even today she still has a complex about herself. Anyway, that's not my problem anymore.

THE ACCIDENT

$\mathcal{I}$ reckon most people have once or twice been in some kind of an accident, even if it was just falling off a bike. So many different types of accidents can happen. We as human beings are subject to a number of different types of accidents, and there are many ways of classifying the different types. Today, a motor vehicle accident occurs every second. Auto accidents cause an injury every 14 seconds, and every 13 minutes a car accident results in a fatality. But why do accidents happen? Some ignorant people might say "Shit happens, but we carry on." To me, that is the most stupid thing I've ever heard, how about you? We humans are programmed not by the Lord, but by man, to learn how to prevent accidents and/or who to turn to if you are involved in an accident (insurance companies, lawyers, etc.). All of us wish to live in and raise our children in safe communities. We find it hard to believe that tragic and traumatic events can happen to us, the people we love, neighbours, peers, and our communities. However, as careful and protective as we try to be, tragic/traumatic events do occur and often take us by surprise, impacting on our lives and the lives of those we are concerned about.

A common feature of all tragic and traumatic events is that they do not happen on a daily basis. Most of us expect to get up in the morning, go to work school or become involved in some other daily activity. There is a familiar routine to our days and we become comfortable with that.

Such events are often outside the range of normal experiences for most of us. Therefore the reactions (thoughts, feelings and behaviour) that they produce may also be outside of what we experience on a daily basis.

Secondly, because many of these accidents result in losses, those impacted can experience intense feelings of grief at the same time as they are dealing with trauma. Afterwards, we may see or experience shock or disbelief. It may be hard to accept that something tragic has occurred. In fact, a state of shock can be helpful. After a severe physical injury, our mind and body go into a state of shock, because if we were to experience all of the pain at once, it could be damaging. After a tragedy, shock and denial allows those affected to slowly absorb the reality of the emotionally painful event. If we were to absorb all the pain at once it could be further damaging. Intense feelings of anger/rage, sadness, guilt, fear, anxiety, shame and/or blame. Because these feelings can change rapidly and become intense, those impacted can fear that they are going 'crazy'. They may experience problems with sleep and appetite, nightmares or feel unconnected with others. They may have physical aches and pains not due to injury (chronic pains is a good example), or have flashbacks of scenes connected with the tragic event. It is important to recognise that these feelings, although extremely unpleasant, are normal reactions to an abnormal event. With appropriate coping skills, support, and time, many of these reactions will eventually decrease or disappear.

Many factors affect how quickly individuals, families and communities recover. These factors include the nature of the tragedy, how many people are impacted, availability of services and supports, belief systems, rituals and coping skills. In my case, the families were not there, only my ex-girlfriend Violet. But the community was wholly behind me. Before I get deeper into details about how and when, let me explain what I am suffering from at the moment. It is called Spinal Cord Injury. With help from my resources, I will explain it in detail. You might ask yourself what Spinal Cord Injury is. Well, a spinal cord injury disrupts communication between the brain and other parts of the body, causing loss of certain functions to cease. Injuries can occur at any level along the spinal cord.

There are thirty-three vertebrae located along your backbone: seven cervical vertebrae in the neck; twelve thoracic vertebrae in the upper back; five lumbar vertebrae in the lower back; five fused sacral vertebrae in the hip area; four fused vertebrae in the coccyx or tailbone.

Spinal cord injuries can occur at any of these levels. The higher up the injury, the more loss of function. The vertebrae are numbered, with number one being at the top. Therefore, a cervical-4 or C-4 injury means the fourth cervical vertebra is damaged, and a thoracic-1 or T-1 injury means the first thoracic vertebra is damaged. Cervical injuries are the most severe.

Spinal cord injury is often abbreviated to SCI. Quadriplegia means the person has limited movement in both the arms and the legs. Paraplegia means only the person's lower body movement is affected. Injuries at the cervical level generally cause quadriplegia. Injuries at the thoracic level usually cause paraplegia.

Spinal cord injuries occur as a result of damage or trauma to the spine. This includes injury to the spine itself or to surrounding tissue or bone, which then may press against the spine. The majority of injuries occur in the cervical region of the spine, which is the neck. About one-third occur in the area where the ribs are attached to the spine. The remaining injuries occur in the lower back.

Having explained a little about the structure of the body, I will now relate what happened to me. It was a summer's day on the 29th of June 1997. My family and I were living in Fürth, Germany. As a matter of fact we had just moved into a new flat. On the 19th of June, 1997, the night before the accident, my girlfriend and I were bar-hopping, until, I suppose, around 5pm. knowing that we had little children alone at home, we then decided it would be the best to go home. Also, the sun was beginning to rise and neither of us had slept for over 24 hours. My intention was that my girlfriend should be the first to go to bed, and I would take care of the children, with breakfast and so on. Around 2pm, I would wake her and she would take over, so that I could lie down. But it didn't work out that way because I went to the cinema with my two boys to see the movie *Batman*. Later on, around 5pm, we were returning home with my friend Boris, with whom I used to work at the Grand Hotel where he was a chef cook, and sometimes he does chauffeuring. And there we became good friends. His ex-girlfriend Silvia was like a sister to me. They had been together over six years, but had recently broken up. That was difficult for Boris to deal with. Anyway, he called me to find out if I had any plans for the evening. I told him that I was feeling very tired because me and my girlfriend had been out the night before out and just got home that morning. I had planned, I explained, to stay at home and watch the boxing match between Mike Tyson and Evander Holyfield. So we agreed he should come over to my home in one hour's time then go to the service station and get a couple bottles of wine, and maybe a six-pack of beer. Then we could watch the boxing match together. Within an hour Boris had arrived. Knowing that the next day we had a long journey ahead of us. You see, that was one of his problems, he drove too fast. I often argued with him because of it. Once we went to the bordering city, Erlangen, which was about 15 kilometres away. I think we made it there in a few minutes whereas normally it would have taken 15-20 minutes. And the greatest risk was my children and Vivian's little girl Michelle was in the car. But for all that, he was good hearted which is why he attracted the sympathy of so many people. The next morning As we were about to depart to the service station for our journey to South Tirol.

South Tyrol is a place where Austria and Italy collide. The magical Alpine region of South Tyrol is a perfect marriage of romance and design. Italian and German cultures do not, as a rule, have many characteristics in common – as anyone who is interested in economics, food or football well knows. This dichotomy makes the Alpine region of South Tyrol an intriguing, Channel 4-style experiment. A geopolitical Wife Swap, if you like. A small, hilly place about twice the size of Kent, South Tyrol is an idyllic enclave of medieval castles, steeple churches, apple orchards and vineyards. An Austrian territory for eons, it has been an Italian province since the First World War, but no one seems to have told most of the half-million inhabitants. I have been here often to take photos for a travel agency catalog. I called home to inform my kids that we would be coming home a little later than planned. Then my son Harold pleaded with me to come home now because he had a bad feeling that something is not right. If only I had heeded his words. Time dragged but eventually it was 5 am and we were still on the interstate. Knowing the fact that we haven't slept that much at all. By now, I insisted that I should drive because Boris has been driving many hours. But he refused. "No one drives my baby!" I knew that it was impossible to convince someone who is totally tired, so I considered getting out of the car at the next filling station, to call my boss. However, I was afraid for Boris, that he would be involved in an accident. That's why I stayed in the car. We ended up at a service station, where Boris began to buy red bull and coffee. I shouted at him and tried to convince him to let me drive or we shall take an hour break. But we were under pressure for time. My boss did not like it, when we come late to an appointment. Getting back in the car was the biggest mistake I ever made – then again maybe it was my fate, my destiny. Anyway, I was sitting in the front and because he was again driving far too quickly, and under the influence of fatigue, I shouted, "Stop the car! I want to get out!" At the next rest stop, I got out and got into the back seat. Soon after we drove off again, I was so tired I fell asleep; I was told by the police that all three of us, Boris, Maria (journalist) and I, had fallen asleep. I can't give you too much detail about how the accident happened for that reason. The only thing I remember is saying that I have to get home because my kids are alone. 3-4 days later I woke up in the hospital's Intensive Care Unit, and the first person I saw was my now ex-girlfriend Vivian. I think that I was on so much strong medication that I felt no pain at all. Vivian didn't tell me that Boris had died at the scene of the accident. I asked, but she said that he was in another clinic and that Maria had broken her lower jawbone and suffered minor scratches and bruises, but had been released from hospital. Then I noticed someone who had came to visit me, holding a newspaper. I could barely make out the headlines, which stated *26 years old chauffer races to his death.* There was a picture of his car lying on its side; my white shirt, the one I was wearing at the time of the accident, was hanging out of the window. Then I knew what had happened. Afterwards, Boris's new girlfriend came into the room to see me; she was dressed in black, her eyes full of tears. I don't recollect everything she told me, but I realised that Boris had died and he had been buried on the day that I came out of the coma. Why didn't *I* die? I have asked myself that question over and over again and in the next chapter you will read why.

THE DISABILITY

*U*nderstanding and coping with these feelings and emotions is an important part of returning to your highest level of functioning and activities. It is normal to feel depressed and scared during the initial stages of your disability. How you manage this transition in your life will determine your ultimate personal success.

You probably won't be working right now. Whether you loved your job or had a normal degree of discontent, it gave you somewhere to go, a social circle of friends and acquaintances, a sense of usefulness and productivity, a regular pay check. Even if you didn't love your job, it provided structure, daily activity, problems to solve and interaction with others. You were part of the big picture.

When first coping with your disability, your time is filled with new and different challenges – doctor and therapy appointments, things to learn about your insurance and benefits, and people from work stopping by or calling to check up on you.

As the weeks and months go by, things begin to change again. The doctor and therapy appointments may not be as frequent and your friends from work get back into their usual routine. Concerns may start to surface about your finances. Your family structure may change because you are no longer the provider and they have to care for you. Your medical situation may be causing you a great deal of pain and you are left with figuring out how to handle it. You may have many restrictions that you didn't have before. You begin to worry that you may never be productive again.

Everyone's situation is different. Your may still be recovering, but it's not too early to set a timeframe for your return to work and eventually being productive again.

But it could be an entirely different situation. You may no longer have an employer or job to return to. You may not be able to return to the kind of work that you have done in the past because of your physical limitations. You might have a high level of pain that you are going to have to learn to live with.

So a disability can be a temporary setback or it can be a totally life-changing experience. How you choose to cope with it will make the difference. We are all different in our psychological makeup so the nature or the severity of the disability matters little in your individual ability to cope with it. We all know people that function 'normally' and have happy and productive lives despite the fact that we know they are sick or in a great deal of pain.

Remember that your feelings are unique and whatever you are feeling is normal because of the big change that has occurred in your life. But there are times when you may not be able to see the light at the end of the tunnel and feel depressed, sad or confused. Don't be afraid to seek professional counselling to help you through these challenging times. I recall being in the rehabilitation centre and opening my eyes to learn I had damaged my spinal cord so badly I would never be able to walk again. Nor would I be able to move my hands or fingers. My body was paralysed from my chest down and I would have to be taken care of like a newborn baby. The life I had taken for granted was to change. I just couldn't bear the facts anymore and refused to participate in physical therapy. I just wanted to go home to my mother. I reached the stage where I was constantly ill. I developed a kidney infection; the doctors almost gave up on me. I remember the Urology Department preparing the operational procedures. They planned to take out one of my kidneys. I had practically given up and to make things worse I had a fever for more than two days. I remember Violet saying: "Fight, Jamie, fight, please don't give up. Your children need you." But I just didn't want to live any longer.

Then, around 5am, I had two visitors. They appeared before me dressed like biblical Hebrews with long black robes and white scarves covering their heads, right down to their shoulders. I remember they were wearing sandals, their hair was as white as snow and their eyes as green as jade. They stood by my bedside and watched over me. One of them held her hand over my forehead and told me that my time was not yet at hand as the Lord had a mission for me. Then I noticed the other one was praying and she was repeating the Lord's Prayer to me, over and over again. I don't remember everything but I do remember the next morning around 5am as I was in the intensive care unit with the morning nurse, who was checking my temperature gradient. "It's impossible!" she shouted.

The fever had gone and the first words came out of my mouth: "I'm hungry."

She paged the doctor and he too was astonished that my condition had changed so dramatically. I asked the nurse who the two women were that had visited me the evening before. She looked at me and said, "Mr Wallace, no one visited you. You were on very strong medication so perhaps you were only dreaming."

But for me it was not a dream; it was real. I then returned to the room where the other patients were and began to pray, day and night, for repentance and forgiveness for the sins that I had committed over the years. Later I was sent home where I eventually made contact with Rev. Jones and his wife. They would come every Sunday and pray with me, encourage me. They were my new family. Two years on and they have returned to America. I feel as though they took a part of me with them because I feel lonely again. But they left me with the hope of receiving and healing.

How Must I Live?

*H*ow must I live? *And it came to pass that, as he went his way, a certain man said unto the Lord, "I will follow thee whithersoever thou goest."*

And Jesus said unto him, "Foxes have holes, and birds of the air have nests; but the Son of Man hath not where to lay his head." And he said unto another, follow me."

I know that if I want to live an everlasting life, I have to continue to do God's will. I have to live cleanly with a respect for human rights, like the great Martin Luther King Jr. He was a man for our times, like Moses in his day. For God used him to pave a better way, a way of peaceful existence between blacks and whites and a greater degree of freedom. It may have cost him his life but his death was not in vain for he helped change the course of history. I am not great like he was but I posses the same intention. That's my life, that's how I want to live, but I feel like a bird that has broken its wings because I am temporarily grounded. Everything that I say and do, being so faint, is hard to be heard. I have to scream and shout so my words will be heard, like a child pulling on its mother's dress, trying to get attention. But I believe that I will be lifted up again because I want to be and I will be fit for the Kingdom of God and I want to live on. How must I live? Only the Lord knows.

I believe,Giving your life to Jesus and living the Christian life begins with faith and repentance. We must first be clear about who Jesus is and what He has done for us. You must come to a conclusion in your heart that Jesus really is God's Son, and that His death on the cross and resurrection from the dead is what you need to have your sins forgiven and to have right relationship with God.

True faith is always connected to repentance. Repentance is a mental understanding that what the Bible calls sin is wrong, a heartfelt acceptance of what the Bible says about sin (that we should be sorry for our sin and hate it), and a personal decision to turn from it (a renouncing of sin and a decision of the will to reject it and lead a life of obedience to Christ instead).

My Boys

As a divorced and single father of two children, I am often accorded a status just shy of sainthood. "How do you do it?" friends ask, with that mixture of pity and awe that single fathers seems to elicit. I sigh deeply and murmur bravely, "You do what you have to do." There's no question that single father face significant difficulties, not the least of which is financial hardship. And there's no question that kids miss the parent who's not with them. If you've got children, being married is undoubtedly better -- but not at all costs. Being a single father is infinitely preferable to living in a bad marriage, and it even has some things worth celebrating.

If someone were to ask me today about how my boys were keeping I would reply by saying, "Do you mean little Harold and sweet little Michael?" You see, they are now grown up. Harold is 20 and Michael is 17, going on 18, and little Bobby is 7 years old. I don't really know too much about how Harold's keeping because I don't see much of him these days. But it's nothing new. He always forgets who's brought him up for the last 12 years. Maybe one day when he has his own children he'll remember me. It's sad to know that you gave half of your life to your kids, always there when they needed you the most and that you were a father and a friend. But now I'm just a handicap. And my own son does not call or come by to say hello. Instead, he spends time with his mother who years ago left him while she ran after different men.

I remember when I was raising him; he would never leave my side. Even when I went to the rest room, he would sit by the door like a puppy and wait until I was finished. Or if I went out of the house to throw the rubbish away or go shopping, he would always be by my side. Many of my friends use to tease me by saying he stick to me like glue. But I understood him. His mother left him and that hurt him so much it left a scar behind. Or when he was sick, I was there for all his wishes and needs. But now the shoe is on the other foot. I am in need of him because he and his brother are the only family I have here in Germany. Maybe he is still too naive to realize it. But I am in good hands now. I have seen the glory of the Lord come to comfort me. My job has been done. One of my seals was to stay here until my boys were old enough to take care of themselves. He is 20 and will be living in a Clostridium for the next three years – thanks to his mother again, years ago she put him in a special education school for children who are slow in learning. And now this: would you call her someone a perfect when they do such things to their children? At the age of 17, Michael has his own flat whereas Harold is 20 and living in a Clostridium. Thanks again to his mother. As I mentioned before, I was totally against it but what could I do? They took advantage of my situation. But justice will be done. In June next month she will be returning to America to stay forever. Michael has an apartment that he cannot afford, but she signs the contract. So if you want my opinion of the whole situation I would say she's not too clever. Anyway, regardless, I still wish both of my sons all the best. I love them both. Now last but not least I still have little Bobby, he is my heart. I call him the new edition. He is seven years old and has the intelligence of an adult. If he continues the way he is doing he will make something of himself one day. But he too does not have it easy with his mother. I always tell him to continue to be nice to her and pray to the Lord. And one day he will have his way. Then he can visit me anytime he wants. Now you know the way I feel and so do my boys.

MY SOUL WAS RESTORED

*J*esus healed a paralysed man. In addition, he entered into a ship, passed over, and came into his own city. They brought to him a man lying sick on a bed suffering with the palsy: and Jesus seeing their faith said unto the sick of the palsy; Son, be of good cheer; thy sins be forgiven thee.

And, behold, certain of the scribes said within them, this man blasphemed.

And Jesus, knowing their thoughts, said, "Wherefore think ye evil in your hearts?" For which is the easier to say, 'Thy sins be forgiven thee' or to say, 'Arise, and walk?' But that ye may know that the Son of man hath power on earth to forgive sins." Then sayeth he to the sick of the palsy, "Arise, take up thy bed, and go unto thine house."

And he arose, and departed to his house.

But when the multitudes saw it they marvelled and glorified God, which had given such power unto men.

If a frog had wings he would not bump his tail on the ground every time he jumped. In addition, there is no house without a home and when one man is happy the other is sad; and finally, yet importantly, no one wants to be alone. My soul was restored. When I was having the time of my life, drinking, women, fast cars and parties, I did not think of words such as those above. Sometimes, I was having so much fun that I almost forgot to look above to say thank you. It is sad when we have to suffer an ordeal in order to have our eyes opened. To see how precious he can be to us. It took a traffic accident that cost me the most important function of the body, the movement of the hands, legs, feet and the sense of touch, hearing, smell and taste. They have all been damaged. Only about twenty percent of my body works properly. There are many things I cannot do anymore and they are the most important things that keep a person living and moving. The doctors told me I would be dependent on others for the rest of my life. Part of what they said is true, but the most important part of all is my brain. Today, I can think and make decisions on how to run my life even though I have a handicap. Once again I am a single parent bringing up my son. So many miracles are slowly occurring in my life. It is not easy, because Satan constantly tries to intercept my plans. So sometimes he gets to me so deeply that I feel like giving in to him. But I will not. Amen.

THE WORLD TODAY

*M*en occasionally stumble over the truth, but most of them pick themselves up and hurry off as if nothing ever happened: *The World Today*

What is wrong with the world today? Pollution, de-forestation, killing animals, and what is the cause of all this destruction? Overpopulation! There are nearly six billion people in the world today, and these people need space, right? So where do they go? Apparently, they don't care and so they take land from its natural inhabitants. When they do this, what happens to everything else? It all falls apart because they bring destruction. It is argued that the human population on our planet cannot exceed 12 billion. At 12 billion, the earth will contain people and their food: nothing else will have space to exist. Something must be done to protect the world and stop the growth of its population. Don't let the natural world become just a memory!

There are conflicts all over the world. It now seems that no country is immune from war. Terrorism has put an iron grip on every country. They accomplished their goals by destroying the economy and putting great fear in the world. The USA spends billions of dollars on security measures of all kinds and this is an ever increasing expenditure. It cannot continue to spend at this incredible rate.

Because of the heightened security, every segment of our lives is now open to inspections by the government and their subcontractors. Private emails are being read, bank transactions are being monitored, telephone conversations are being listened to and this is just what we know of. You can safely assume they are using satellites to spy on the public. People are being trained to become whistleblowers on their neighbours. All these things are draining hundreds of billions of dollars.

These security measures demand people involved in highly specialised professions. These people are experts in tapping into any kind of information required, anywhere and in countless numbers of ways. This is bad enough but it is greatly compounded by the fact that this gathered information will inevitably be used for corruption sooner or later. This is a certainty because the very people that develop this technology and work with it are themselves corrupt no matter what title is assigned to them. An example is credit card fraud which is rampant because of technology. Disgruntled workers are also to blame for information leakage.

What is especially troubling today is incredible corporate greed and theft. Regularly we hear of corporate scandals and embezzlements. To make it worse, these white collar criminals have learned to steal legally by using the technology available, something which they have mastered to their advantage. Almost every business, large or small, has persons of this mindset to steal in any way they can. They have no moral conscience. Anything goes as long as they make money and don't get caught. And these are just the ones we hear of. How many more are there still uncovered? The numbers must be staggering.

There are now more than a dozen nations, each with its finger on the nuclear button. All it takes is one of them to have a rush of blood and before they know it launch a nuclear weapon. One nuclear blast in a major US city will have effects lasting many, many years. Even to this day, there are still people who are permanently disfigured from the Hiroshima and Nagasaki bombs of 1945. Not to mention those hundreds who later contracted cancer from the radiation and died. The world will be plunged into depths of fear so great it will never recover from it.

There is also great upheaval in the natural world. In Europe, floods have done a colossal amount of damage. The US is plagued by terrible floods, hurricanes and great fires. Earthquakes are common all over the world and are increasing in magnitude. They can be found in places where just a few years ago they were non-existent. The environment is being polluted and destroyed at a incredible rate. Take a look at the rain forests. Plants and animal species are becoming extinct almost daily. Never to live or be seen again. How sad and all because of the ever-increasing greed of man.

Over the past fifteen years people's sense of morality has been at rock bottom. On TV and in movies are scenes of depravity unknown in our parents' generation. Children in their teens and even younger are committing the most horrendous crimes – in some cases murder – without a thought. Much of this is because of their parents who themselves have no moral character. How can they raise moral children? Perverse practices are taught to children and the latter seeing them as being normal and acceptable. These practices are prevalent in schools today. In fact, they are not perverse at all but just another lifestyle. It is now normal for a couple to live together outside of wedlock to see if they can make it or just for economic reasons. This practice is encouraged and accepted by most people and glorified in the media. Perhaps the media and movie industry more than anything else have done most to harm the morals of society and especially those of children,

As discouraging and unpleasant as it is to hear of these things, they will not last forever. Everything mentioned above and more has been foretold by Jesus centuries before.

Today is filled with anger fuelled with hate and the anger of people afraid of sharing a common fate. Today is built on tragedies, for example the war in in Iraq, which no one wants to face. Rage and violence abound, children are bred with hate in their hearts because no one at home cares. Tonight I lay my head but the fear of what the future holds is never ending.

Today is 26th March, 2003. I am sitting outside on my terrace; it is partly cloudy with a light breeze. The sun is shining in my face; the temperature is around 16-17c. The birds are singing, spring is here at last, the flowers are slowly waking from their winter sleep. In three weeks we have Easter, and my garden is already decorated with colorful Easter eggs. As for my health, well, I still have a bladder infection that I have suffered from for over two years. In addition, my doctor is constantly pumping me with antibiotics. I think my body is so resistant to antibiotics that there is no response anymore. My gluteus muscle still needs day-to-day treatment because its takes forever to heal. The question is, will it ever heal again? My son Michael ,is in vocational school today; my assistant Ronny is on vacation. On Thursday, I'll have more time for myself as I don't have any therapy. That's when I take advantage of the spare time to work on my first book.

For 6 days and 12 hours Britain and the United States have continually bombed Iraq,because of weapons of mass destruction. There have been many wounded and killed, most of them children. This is a pointless war. The U.S. so-called Commander-in-Chief did not win the election, but was appointed by the Supreme Court to be president. The panel consisted of seven of the most renowned judges in the country. They voted 5-7 for George Bush. The funny thing about the whole system is that President Bush's father, ex-president George Bush Senior. appointed those seven judges to the Supreme Court. Now here's the thing: two of the seven judges were black. Remember, he won 5-7. I think you get the picture. He is now the president but we won't get into politics,other than that. After all, I'm sure you read the newspapers.

Today is the 23th of November, 2003, nine months on. The war in Iraq is over but there have been hundreds of American soldiers killed on a daily basis. The world is outraged by the conflict and every day, all over the world, there is a demonstration against President Bush. In Saudi Arabia, terrorist groups are bombing on a large scale; wherever, in fact, there are Americans. The cost of living has reached a record high, so has unemployment. Years before Bush became president and the world wasn't in the crital condition it is now, a pack of chocolate chip biscuits would cost 90 cents; today, it costs one dollar and 75 cents. A 12-piece bag of chicken wings would have cost you six dollars and 20 cents, a packet of cigarettes 29 dollars. It costs 1.5 million dollars for each day that Bush keeps American soldiers in Iraq. We have gay couples, lesbians that have the right to marry,and just recently a law was pass that allow a gay Catholic Bishop to continue to work in the Closter and finally they are debating whether or not homosexuals can adopted children. That's the world today. Shall I continue?

Before the second coming of Jesus, the world unrest we have today will continue to grow worse. Known as the tribulation or the time of trouble, there will be no relief from these events until Jesus is seen in the clouds of heaven. There will be no great time of peace and prosperity as men falsely predict today. There will be no great cities of peace on other planets.

Before any significant event takes place in the earth's history, Jesus, through His prophets, His messengers and the Bible will give us signs and warnings so that we may know what will take place and for how long we have to live.

There will be wars and rumors of wars, all the nations will be talking of peace while making ready for war. Natural disasters like floods and hurricanes, earthquakes, terrible crimes, greed of enormous proportions will prevail. Great selfishness and total disregard for others will be the order of the day, Mark 13:7.

As the end of the world draws nearer, all these events will become more frequent and intensify until they are all happening at about the same time. Many will argue that we've always had these things on the earth. True, but the difference is the *frequency* and *intensity* of these events. At no time in history have these things happened as closely together as they are doing today.

We will see the conditions that prevailed in Noah's day. Drinking, marrying and giving in marriage, eating to great excess, total disregard for anything noble. The basest instincts will constantly be on the minds of man and glorified by the media. Every abominable thing will be cherished and practised. Matthew 24:37.

There will be a joining of Church and State. At the present time, government money is helping religious and social organisations. There is a renewed awareness and interest in the ten commandments in government offices. Why is this a bad thing? Because the government cannot legislate religion. They will try to rule by oppression and laws with corresponding penalties.

There will be economic upheaval. Right now, there is talk of a recurrence of the great depression of the 1920s and even worse this time. Insatiable greed is on the minds of many persons in positions of economic control in every company and government worldwide. You can see this happening as great scandals are uncovered where billions are stolen from the people by a few greedy ones. In every business, people look after number one, driving many to commit theft and deception. Selfishness supreme rules the mind of man.

The gospel of the Lord will prevail throughout the world. As a result of the Internet, the gospel has been spread to every part of the globe for the first time in history. The gospel has now reached all the world. Jesus said when the gospel is in all the world, then the end will come.

As world conditions become worse and worse, people throughout the world will feel a great sense of hopelessness and despair. Finally, people will welcome any remedy for these conditions. Even today, people are readily accepting patriotic acts in the hope of averting further acts of terrorism.

In an attempt to relieve these terrible conditions, the apostate churches will suggest a re-institution of the Sunday Laws*. God, they will reason, must be very angry and causing all these terrible things to happen on the earth. They will claim that the way to please God is by returning to church on Sundays. And so this Sunday Law will be put into effect.

Even after the Sunday law has been put into place, there will be many who at first do not obey it. This first institution of the law will be a strong suggestion only – something very similar to how the laws against cigarette smoking began.

They will see the terrible conditions continue and come to the conclusion that it is the fault of all those who do not obey the law that God is still angry. And they will make the law mandatory to obey. At the same time, the law will become universal throught the world.

And she (the USA) will make all nations follow after the beast*: Revelation 14:8.

With the law now greatly strengthened by being backed with civil penalties, most of those who previously offended will obey and submit to the law. Except, that is, for the small number who follow all of God's commandments. For following this oppressive law means denying the true God and paying homage to a pagan, a false god (the word Sunday comes from the pagan sun god).

This small group of God's remnants will be rooted out and brought before the civil courts to answer for their crime against the Sunday Law. They will be imprisoned and fined for disobeying, just as a common criminal is treated today. The whole of civilisation will be bitterly opposed to the small group. An amendment to the law will state that those who oppose the Sunday law will not be able to buy or sell any goods. Many of the trade unions will help to facilitate this blockade since they control most of the commerce.

Even with these harsh measures in place, the apostate churches and the government will not be able to do anything to make the small group recant and obey the Sunday Laws. And the terrible conditions in the world will continue.

As a last resort, a decree will be added to the effect that whoever disobeys the law will be executed as, they will argue, the only way to save many is to sacrifice a few. At this very time, such a way of thinking is alive in the world. Laws are emerging that tackle anything that is considered harmful to society; for instance, environmental toxins, smoking, child predators, even hateful and not so hateful speech and particularly anything racial. This same attitude will drive on the Sunday laws because the governments will decide a small company is harming society by disobeying the Sunday law and thereby bringing God's wrath upon them.

Right up to the present day, the pleas for mercy continue in the form of the third angel's messages given by the persecuted remnant. This will be the last message given to an evil world, totally deceived and overcome by Satan: Revelation 14:9.

When the Sunday law is enforced accompanied by a death decree, the law of God will have been made totally null. Little does man know that he will have offended God to the limit by voiding His fourth commandment and persecuting His remnant. His cup of indignation will have grown full and God will no longer allow this to continue. God will now come out of His place to put a end to the wicked inhabitants of earth: Revelation 14:10.

After the giving of the third angel's message, probation will close. Then it won't make any difference whether or not a person accepts God. The time of forgiveness is finally over. Nothing a wicked man says or does from this point will gain him salvation: Revelation 22:11. God exchanges His priestly attire for that of a King and assumes the role of Judge.

When the world reaches this stage, the time to the second coming of the Lord can be measured in weeks: Revelation 16:1-17.

As God did in the land of Egypt long ago, so once again plagues will fall upon the earth. The only difference is that the second coming will immediately follow these plagues. The first plague was grievous sores on all those who trampled on the seventh-day Sabbath and received the mark of the beast. There is no relief from these sores.

In the second plague, the seas will turn to blood. This is for the blood of the saints taken by the beast. Water can support life no longer. The third plague will be the inland waters of lakes and rivers turning to blood. There will be no more clear, fresh water anywhere in the world. The fourth plague will scorch man by the sun getting many times hotter.

Note that the wicked are still trying to hunt down and kill the remnant at this point. It seems to the remnant God has left them as wicked men are about to gain victory over them. Then the fifth plague will take place. Darkness will fall upon the earth. This will stop the wicked in their tracks. They will be gripped with fear. They will have forgotten about hunting down the small companies of the remnant. During the sixth plague the support for the beast will dry up. Unfortunately, it's much too late for any of them. Probation has long closed. The heavens will open and close like a scroll. Black clouds will cover the entire sky and rumblings are heard throughout the earth.

Finally there will be seventh plague. The greatest earthquake in the history of the earth will take place. Mountains will literally be moved out of their places and flattened. The seas will boil with much turbulence, boulders will be thrown out of them. At the same time, great hailstones, each weighing 57 pounds, will rain from the heavens. These hail stones will level the mightiest structures of man. Just as in the temple of old

Jerusalem, not one stone will be left atop another, so complete will be the destruction. There will be nothing of man still functional. Man will have nowhere to hide. It is now just God and man alone.

During this seventh and last plague, amid the thunder and lightning, there will in the east be a small black cloud about half the size of a man's hand. Immediately, the small and hated companies will know this is the sign of the coming of the Son of Man and their fear will be replaced by great relief, hope and joy. At this time, a hand will appear in the heavens holding the ten commandments written in stone. The fourth commandment of the seventh-day Sabbath observance is clearly pointed out. Suddenly, the wicked world that was about to kill all of God's true remnants see they have been fighting against God by enforcing a false, pagan Sunday. They now see they were Satan's disciples, terribly deceived and ready to carry out the killing of God's remnant people. They now see clearly they have been worshipping a false, pagan day. They realise it was man driven by Satan who changed the true seventh-day Sabbath of the fourth commandment to a pagan Sunday. They turn their despair and rage upon the false apostate ministers who guided them towards this path of destruction by using smooth, lying words of 'peace and safety': 1 Thess. 5:3.

The small black cloud, now much larger, draws ever nearer the earth and the form of Jesus can clearly be seen. The cloud turns out to be billions of angels. The radiance of glory is now so overpowering to the wicked that they desperately look for cover among the rocks and caverns of the earth. The remnant of God sees the procession in a clear, comfortable, warm light. To the wicked, the glory of God is a consuming fire. To the saints, it is a warm and pleasant light, the love of God.

While probation was still open, they were given every chance to hear the truth and turn to the true God. But they rejected it all and chose the temporal enticements and pleasures of the world instead of accepting the life-giving message of the true God. Now it's all far too late. Most damage on earth can be repaired but this is not the case now. There is no shelter they can retreat to, just the pronouncement of the final judgment. As the heavenly procession draws ever nearer the earth, the heavenly glory consumes the wicked and they are all destroyed, for evil cannot exist in the presence of a Holy God. They are not buried but cast the length and bredth of the earth, strewn about like refuse.

Just before the priests, rulers and Roman soldiers crucified Jesus, Jesus' last words to them were, "Thou hast said: nevertheless, I say unto you, Hereafter shall ye see the Son of Man sitting on the right hand of power, and coming in the clouds of heaven": Matt 26:64. So they now stood speechless, looking into the piercing gaze of Him whom they called a blasphemer and a liar. The Roman soldiers and Pilate see the nail prints in Jesus' hands and they all know they crucified the Son of God. They recall those last words of Jesus ever so clearly. Gone is that crown of thorns and the stripes from the whip. Instead, they stand before the King of Kings and Lord of Lords, the Saviour who pleaded with them to accept God. Having fulfilled His promise to them, Jesus again returns them to dust to await the second resurrection of the condemned and the judgment.

Jesus then calls forth all those that have died in His name from the beginning of creation. Countless millions come forth in immortal glory, never to die again, to a new life of eternal happiness. The small company are now fully lit with God's glory and they too assume immortality. Angels go forth to all corners of the earth gathering His redeemed, bringing to mothers long-departed children, uniting long lost relatives. All the raised righteous and living righteous begin their upward journey toward Heaven where they will spend the next 1000 years with Jesus. This is the first resurrection of the righteous.

The earth will be totally destroyed. Nothing is left but darkness and destruction, the once looming skyscrapers and monuments of proud man are not to be seen nor will they ever be seen again. Bound to this scene of utter destruction, this will be Satan's home for the next 1000 years. No one to tempt, a thousand years to think about the result of rebellion and the coming judgment day.

For the next millennium, the saints live with God in heaven. This is a period of adjustment where all the questions of the saints are answered. There will be many questions. Why did a certain person not make it? Why is this or that husband not present. Some wives and relatives are not there. Children are not seen. They seemed so good on earth, why are they not here? Did God make a mistake? To answer these questions, the saints get to see the 'books' of God. They now see where Jesus and the angels pleaded with that person endlessly. Yet they rejected the pleadings. Their hearts were hardened. Many even knew the truth but neglected to accept it into their lives. Many put it off to another day, another time. There are those who professed the word of God and attended church regularly. But still they did not live the word of God in their lives. For if they truly loved the Lord, they would have delighted in spreading the gospel. They did not do this. Yes, they gave tithe, they worked hard at functions, many knew a great deal about the Bible. On the outside, they seemed like Christians but they were Christians in name only. They only performed the easy duties for their Lord. They were too busy with the world to give God much of their time. They did not have the vital, personal, friendship with Jesus necessary for salvation. They did not know Jesus, and likewise Jesus did not know them. So many will be lost in this manner: Matthew 7:21.

After looking at God's books of record, all the redeemed will be satisfied with God's judgment as to why certain persons didn't make it. All questions are now answered beyond all doubt and they find God was indeed totally just and accurate. They fully accept this decision for the rest of eternity. And this sorrowful memory will be wiped from their minds.

After the millennium, all the angels and the redeemed in Heaven descend back to earth with the Holy City. People's final home will be here where the present earth is now, not far away in heaven as many think in gross error. Thus the passage, 'The meek will inherit the earth' (Mark 5:5) is literally true. The Holy City will descend to earth, but before it touches down, Jesus calls forth all the wicked who have died since creation. They all come forth and their numbers are as the sands of the sea. Countless millions. But unlike the saints who were raised perfect in immortal glory, the wicked come up in the same decrepit, sorry condition as when they died. Disfigured from disease, war and accidents, a loathful scene. They retain the original, sinful state of mind they had at death. Murderers will again be murderers. Thieves will again think of stealing. This is the resurrection of the wicked.

With these huge numbers of wicked again living, Satan sees he has a huge army. Thoughts of conquering and evil plots once again fill his mind. He convinces the countless wicked they can overtake the city of God and eat of the tree of life within to gain immortality and so they begin to fashion implements of war. In this huge group are generals, mighty men, warriors, kings, captains who never knew defeat down the ages.

Then with Satan leading, the huge army marches toward the city of God. Jesus closes the gates and the saints go to the top wall of the Holy City. From atop the wall, Jesus tells the wicked below to behold the reward of the righteous as He points to the saints with their crowns and immortal beauty. Then He faces the saints and tells them to behold the reward of the wicked. At this moment, fire rains down from the heavens and begins consuming the wicked.

When Jesus has to destroy His children who would not accept Him and chose Satan instead, He does so with the greatest of sorrow and grief. He would have much rather brought them into the Holy City and given them immortality too. But they rejected His endless pleas and so they chose to be destroyed. It is greatly misunderstood that the destruction of the wicked is God's act of mercy. Those that chose to live in a life of sin, would not be happy in Heaven where perfect righteousness exists. They would not be able to adjust. They would strive to continue in sin. So God has no choice but to do His 'strange act' of mercifully destroying them.

When the wicked have been burnt, this fire continues in order to to purify the earth. When all the remnants of the old earth are burnt, the fire goes out and the earth is now new again as it was at the creation. There is no trace whatsoever of the old earth and the wickedness that prevailed there before. At last, God has a clean universe again. Once purified, the earth is now ready to receive the Lord and the Holy City. When Jesus' feet touches the Mount of Olives, it becomes a great plain, beyond what the eye can see. The Holy City descends to this great plain and settles into permanent place. On this new earth, the saints of God reign and live on forever. They will mature in stature as man was originally created in Eden. Man's intellect will again be restored fully. He will once again be taught of God. All the creations of God will be open for the inspection and enjoyment of His saints. God Himself will explain all questions. In the new earth, there will be no more night but eternal day. There will be no need of the sun for the glory of God will provide eternal light and warmth.

Where will you be?

Now, the biggest question of all. Will you be ready when Jesus comes again? He gave each of us this opportunity to be one of His children by taking our sins upon Himself and dying on the cross. All you have to do is accept that He is creator of all things and believe in Him. Most of all, have Him as a personal, daily friend and saviour. Just you and Jesus. Then, when you see Him, it will be like finally seeing an old friend. It's as simple as that.

*Sunday Laws or blue laws are already on the books of many states in the USA. They just have to be activated and updated. Briefly, they state no one is to operate a business on Sunday and that they should attend church. This Sunday law becomes oppressive when compliance becomes mandatory on punishment of fine and imprisonment.

** What is the mark of the beast? Bible scripture, Revelation 14:9. A person gets the mark of the beast by worshipping a pagan Sunday instead of the true, fourth commandment Sabbath. The mark of the beast is not a physical mark of any kind. It simply means all those who choose to follow a pagan, false worship day instead of the true Sabbath of God's fourth commandment. Receiving the mark of the beast applies to the time of decision when the choice will be given as to who to follow, God or man. None as of yet has the mark of the beast. It happens during the tribulation of the last days.

On the Sabbath

The true, seventh-day Sabbath of the fourth commandment is most important to God. It is His memorial day to celebrate the creation of the world. Observance of this fourth commandment Sabbath is important to God, man's loyalty to God depends on it. In the final account, man's salvation hinges on it's observance or non-observance. These are the two classes that will exist in the last days just before the second coming of Jesus.

But tomorrow I hope to wake and see changes, a chance to build belief in the form of spiritual intent of the heart and ideals based on truth and tomorrow. I shall wake with a second wind, strong and proud to know I fought with all my heart to keep my dream alive.

OH, MY GOD!

I cried out in pain. And when I realised what had happened, I began to shake in disbelief. Then a question occurred to me but I didn't want to ask the doctors so I asked myself instead. Is this a nightmare? I tried to get out of bed then gazed around the room but it was hard to see my surroundings, mainly because I was lying flat on my back. The next moment my girlfriend put her hands gently on my head and stroked me almost absentmindedly as if she was consoling herself over my death. Dr Brockhammer, was sitting at the dressing table reviewing my x-rays and constantly glancing at me. I remember she was wearing a gold chain on her wrist. She suddenly sat on the side of my bed. It was difficult for me to relax as I feared I was to be given bad news. Suddenly, all was silent. She was wearing her surgery uniform with a white hospital coat. At that moment nothing appeared to be out of the ordinary. She begin to explain to me that I had been involved in a very serious accident and had been undergoing surgery for more then seven hours. She added that it had been a very delicate and complicated operation. As she continued, I felt a cold breeze, she must have felt it too as she stared at the closed window. Then she resumed and gravely informed me that I would be unlikely to walk or use my hands again. She stepped back a little and the only thing I could see was a black silhouette against the softly lighted room. Then I swallowed slowly and tried to compose myself and say something or ask her a question. But I didn't. I couldn't. "Get out!" I shouted.

My Seal

*W*hen we hear the word 'seal' we automatically think of the final chapter, the end, the final touch. The seal. The sign and the seal. In mediaeval times, in the 16th century, people would close confidential or top secret documents with a seal, to make sure it would not be opened or meddled with should it fall into the wrong hands. Well, I find this difficult to say. This is the closing chapter of my life because my life sometimes feels like a story, a never-ending story but a story just the same. I want you to know that the struggle, the trials and tribulations will continue as long as I am alive and beyond.

A long time ago, an American patriot, named Patrick Henry, went in the history books when he said: "Gentlemen may cry peace, peace, but there will be no peace, give me liberty or give me death." Well I cannot promise you that I will go down in the history books, but I hope that my words will be heard all over the world in every language, because I believe this is a small part of God's mission, something that I have to do. My life is not over and I will continue, although I must confess it's not easy to write a book. I don't understand how the stars write an autobiography in two weeks. And why it took me around two years to get this far.

So now you see who is really writing and who lets other people write for them. So far, I think you all know me pretty well, you know my pro's and con's, but did I mention what I like to eat? Well, I'm not a choosy person. I am thankful for what I get. I mean, I don't eat everything I see. I just eat to nourish my body. I used to drink on occasions; for instance, if I was in a good mood or with good friends. My favorite drink was Tequila, which I learnt about when I was in Mexico, and I learnt about beer here in Germany. That's because the beer here in Germany is consider an nutrition. I used to smoke too. Well, I used to. I started when I came to Germany and I am going to let you in on a little secret. I am 45 years old, and my father still does not know that I used to smoke. Can you keep such secret from your family? How do I dress? I love to dress well because you never know what might happen. For instance, I was once in a situation in which I was wearing non-matching socks and on my way to work. As I was about to cross the intersection on my bike a car suddenly hit me. I fell onto the street, but nothing happened to me. Suddenly, people were gathering round and shortly afterwards the ambulance arrived. At that moment I was not concerned whether or not I was injured; my main worry was that someone would notice I was wearing non-matching socks! So although that might sound a little frivolous it's one reason why dressing well is always important to me. Take women as another example; most of them would never leave the house before putting on their makeup!

There's so many people I would like to tell you about; people who sometime, somewhere meant something to me. So what I've decided to do is to tell you about a few of them. First, I will begin with my physical therapy lady Hannah. She has been treating me for a little over three years now. She's a very nice and quiet young lady. She is a vegetarian and has a cat named Pauline, her boyfriend is a lawyer. She is a very good listener. I tell her about all of my day-to-day activities. She also gives me good tips; all in all, I feel that Hannah is a good mentor.

Gladys, comes from Brazil and is full of fire. She is also very, very sweet. Sometimes she works for me and, believe me, I love every minute of her company. She is marry to a wonderful man, the sort of man every woman dreams of.

Angela, is a very beautiful little girl whom I have known since she was two. Today she is 15 yrs old. I think that I will include her in my last will and testament. She is the child of Jeffery and Carmen who are proud of their little daughter.

I must mention Jeffery, someone I met one night back in 1997 in a local dance club called Rocky Mountain. It was an international club. We became good friends, but because I was living in the next town, Fürth, I didn't see him that often. But I will never forget after I woke up out of my coma that the first person I saw other than my girlfriend was Jeffery. Every day he would visit me and bring me food from McDonald's. Over the years our friendship has developed and we are now very close. Today, I gave him the job of helping me to get into bed. His wife Carmen, whom I've know since around 1983, used to be my neighbor. She is nice and very helpful. Then we have Anje, whom I met in the rehabilitation centre in Garmisch, Germany. Anje was 18 back then and is now 22, married and has a four-month-old child. We have the same type of handicap, Spinal Cord Injury (Tetraplegia). But she is more mobile than I am. I met her in the cafeteria. It was funny because we started to blow grape seeds at each other. Okay, I know it's a crazy way to get to know someone! Soon we began chatting to each other and very soon we became good friends and still keep in contact with each other today.

Another close friend is Ronny who works for me Monday through to Friday. Recently, she met a man on the Internet and they've fallen in love. I think that they spend as much time together as possible. Indeed, they went on a four weeks cruise recently. Ronny is a single mother with twins, and the twins are her A & O. She is also the sort of person you can really depend on. Whenever I was in a tight situation she would always be there. We would have our bad days but in the long run she was a good friend.

The Rev. Jones and Coleen were like a mother and father to me. I respect them very much, because through their comfort and prayers they helped me to wake and see the light of life again. God sent them to me, and I will never forget them. They left Germany in 2002 and I miss them so much. I lost contact with them but I know that one day I will see them again. Other than my boys, these people also mean a lot to me.

Here are a few other good friends: Tillman and Lena are siblings, friends like those are very hard to find. I love both of them, and hope that the Lord will always pave a clear road for them. And for all the others, Thomas, Mona, and Mahag, Stephan and their twins, and many, many more. I wish them all the best, and hope that they will be chosen to enter the gates of Heaven.

However, I'm slightly upset about one of my boys, Harold. Since March of 2003 he has not called or visited me as since then he has been in contact with his mother again. But it doesn't worry me that much because I know I did not do anything to him, and I imagine that he has a guilty conscience. And I still love him because he is my first born child. Michael move out on April 30, 2003. I was totally against it but his mother had persuaded him so much that my efforts to make him stay were futile. But he comes to visit me just about every evening. And my little Bobby comes every 14 days. He wants to live with me so I am still having disputes with his mother over the affair. She hates me and she is a very brittle and wicked woman. But I do not understand why she acts like that towards me. She left me for another man and she has had a child with him, so that's three altogether. But with different men of course. She hates her ex-husband the same as me. And we cannot understand why she thinks we treated her so bad and why she blames us. Today, she is the one that is not happy with her life but still I do not wish any harm to befall on her and i pray for her in the hope that one day she will fall to her knees and ask for forgiveness.

My Closing Remarks

I want to thank each and everyone who bought and read ,my very first book. I hope you enjoyed it because if so it will make me very happy. Maybe we will meet someday. Please remember the things I went through to survive and have faith in God because without faith it is impossible to please Him; for he that cometh to God must believe that he is and that he will reward those that diligently seek him.

See you soon and may God bless you all.

Special thanks go to: Veronica Schilling, Claudia Sickel, Martina Aschoff, Sabine, Reiner Schweizer, Christian and Anje Kill, Peter Kunecke, Michael and Terry Batten, Gabi Seubert, Aexl Bauer, Livi Fedorova and Family, My sisters and Brother and many, many more.

May 15, 2007